Stories, Long & Short is a menagerie
of sagas, legends, accounts, and tales
written by Alberto Arcia. They are
designed to expose the reader to the
writer's uninhibited madness. These
stories were penned in different genres to
display the mood of the author and to
express his feelings about life, women,
and places.

Although many of the stories are purely
fictional, some are based on real people,
places, and events. Names have been
changed to protect the privacy of those
involved, and details have been
elaborated for entertainment purpose.

*'The truth in its purest form is boring, which is why fiction was
invented.' - Arcia*

1

Published through Create Space

Cover Design by Robyn Arcia

Para Keila con Cariño

'Man who lays woman on top of hill, not level.'

Old Chinese/Panamanian proverb.

Confucius might have said it; Redd Foxx did say it.
– Arcia says it all the time.

In Memory of John Smith

You were the only other person I knew that had to show his driver's license in order to confirm his name. I miss your laughter, your sense of humor, and your friendship.

Table of Contents

Special thanks go to Paul Bussard for his help on this project.

Thanks also to Betsy. Your silent support is appreciated.

Stories, Long & Short

By

Alberto Arcia

In the dry season of 1975 and again in 1978, the author drove from Houston to Panama. During both journeys he ran across a number of colorful individuals. He also had to deal with a few unpleasant incidents. Arcia included most of the incidents, and some of the characters into his first novel. "Cut and Run - The Misadventures of Alex Perez." The story of Don Pedro's Cow is a chapter in that book, and it won first place in a short story competition sponsored by The Woodlands Writers Guild. It is included in their 2015 Anthology. The story of Don Pedro's Cow is **Rated PG**

Don Pedro's Cow

"Another damn forest, second one today. Except for the lack of mountains, this place reminds me of the northwest."

Ramona smiled and gave me a kiss on the cheek. "I can't wait to get to Panama. I hope your mother approves of me."

No chance in hell. She will have a heart attack when she takes a gander at your clothing style. "Me too," I said.

"It would be nice if you two could stop kissing and find me a toilet," said Charlene, my soon to be mother-in-law. I have to pee, bad."

I looked at her through the rear-view mirror. "We're in Mexico, for God's sake. There are no rest stops along the highways. Try to cut down on the beer drinking. Your bladder would appreciate it. I know I will."

"Up yours, Alex," said the old bear. "Find me a bathroom or I'm pissing in a beer can."

I cowered at the thought. *Mom's not going to like her either. Charlene's personality resembles a badger in heat.*

I have asked myself, several times, why I'm marrying into this family. The answer is always the same: Charlene is loaded, and Ramona has a body to die for. She also likes to put-out a lot, and for a guy with my take on life, that was enough. Besides, the level of hostility that is going to come out of both families would give the new marriage a good balance.

Ramona began to check the road map. "It looks like we're eighty miles from San Cristobal De Las Casas," she said.

"I can't wait that long," growled the grizzly.

When she reached down to get an empty can, I panicked and pulled over.

"Can you pee in the woods?"

She shot me the bird and climbed out of the car.

***

On the third day of our journey we broke the first rule to do with safety, we picked up a couple of young Mexican urchins that were hitchhiking. Their names were Junior and Raúl.

Right off the bat, I peg the older kid for a scoundrel. The youngest one had a sense of innocence about him, but he could not speak. He was mute.

Junior told us they were going to visit their uncle in Merida. Then he asked me where we were heading.

I measured my words carefully. "The purpose of this trip, besides tourism, is to unite me and Ramona in matrimony. We are driving to Panama so we can do it with both our mother's present."

He gave me a big smile.

Needing to feed my sense of curiosity, I asked him where the name Junior came from.

"My father gave it to me," he said.

The females loved the answer, and had a good chuckle.

I cringed, the scruffy kid had gotten a laugh at my expense. That didn't set well. Not wanting to give him the last verbal jab, I continued with my inquiry. "I want to know the name of your father," I demanded.

He looked at me with suspicion. "Why do you want to know?"

"Leave him alone," growled the old abominable woman. "What is it to you, anyway?"

I looked at Junior and asked him again. "What's your father's name?"

He thought about it for a moment, then came up with an absurd answer. "My father is Jimmy Buffet, the American singer. "My name is Jaime Buffet, but he calls me Junior."

The females laughed again.

"Oh, give me a break," I said. "You don't expect us to believe that load of crap, do you?"

"Watch your mouth, Alex," said Ramona.

"Give the kid a break," growled Charlene. "What's with you today?"

Junior opened his back-pack, rummaged through it, pulled out an old photo and handed it to Charlene.

She looked at it and laughed. "That's Jimmy Buffet all right. Who is the woman with him?"

"It's my mother. That's a photo of my father and mother."

Charlene passed it to Ramona, and she laughed when she saw it. "I guess the kid showed you, uh? That's twice he's got you. You want to try for three?"

Before I could come up with a reply, Ramona cut me off at the pass. She gave the photo to me, and followed the action with a stern voice. "Look at it, apologize, and leave the boy alone."

Shit, that's him all right, probably *nothing more than a photo between the singer and a fan.* I gave it back, mumbled a quick "I'm sorry," and dropped the subject.

***

The drive was long. Ramona, Charlene, and Raúl succumbed to the rhythm of the road, and slept. Junior remained awake. The scraggly kid kept looking at me from the back seat. An hour down the road, I looked at the gas gauge and frowned. *Shit, we're about to run out of gas.*

Junior must have seen my uneasiness because he asked me, "Is everything all right, Mister Alex?"

"No, everything is not all right, we're about to run out of gasoline."

As soon as I said it, the engine sputtered and died. I looked for a place to pull over, and we coasted to a stop.

Junior and I volunteered to hitchhike with the empty five-gallon container, but Ramona and Charlene objected. They were nervous about being left alone on the side of the road with a car loaded with General Electric merchandise that I had bought for my mother.

I told Junior he needed to stay with them, but that didn't set well with him. He wanted to go with me.

"Getting gas is a man's job," he said.

"I know. That's precisely why I'm going. You need to stay here and protect the women."

He looked at me and crossed his arms. "What can I do against armed bandits? I'm just a kid?"

We were discussing who would stay behind when an old man with two kids in tow approached us.

"Buenos días," he said, tipping his sombrero. "I'm Pedro Ávila, and these two handsome boys are my grandsons, Antonio and

11

Armando."

The boys grinned and removed their hats.

"You cannot stay here for very long," said the old guy. "This is dangerous for you, too many bad people on the road. You need to come with me. I will offer you my home until you can fix the problem with your car."

We conferred and accepted his offer. The talk about armed bandits had spooked the women.

Charlene asked Pedro if there was any way we could tow the car to a safer place. He told her not to worry, he knew where there was an ox that could be harnessed to pull the car.

Charlene asked if we could borrow it.

The old man smiled. Then, with an apologetic tone, told her that it could not be borrowed, but it could be rented.

In no time at all we found ourselves in a small but neat cinderblock house. It wasn't far from where we were stranded, and that pleased us. Raúl made friends with Antonio and Armando. Junior stayed by my side.

It didn't take us long to notice an empty food pantry. How to accept Pedro's hospitality without becoming a burden became a source of concern for us.

Charlene wanted to offer the old man money for our room and board, but I didn't want to offend him by offering to pay for what he had offered for free. Still, we needed to find a way to put money in his pocket so food could be purchased. Looking around the place, I noticed there was a cow tied in the backyard. I told Pedro that we were grateful for the offer to spend the night, but first we needed to take care of the vehicle.

"Yes, you are right," he said. "Let me get my sombrero and I will take you to the man who owns the ox."

"Listen Don Pedro, instead of doing business with him, I rather do business with you. It's getting late, and unless you have a problem with the idea, I want to rent your cow. She seems sturdy enough to help us pull the car. Charlene wants us to do it now, and the distance is not too far. What do you say? Can we rent the cow you have in the backyard?"

He scowled at the suggestion.

Wanting to cut off any escape route the old man might come up with, I mentioned that in view of the fact there was no woman in the house, my wife was honor bound by her Texas culture to cook for all of us.

He smiled.

I asked him if there was a store nearby, because the women wanted to go and buy some special ingredients. "Ramona wants to cook a Texas style meal for you and your boys," I said. "You are in for a treat because she is an excellent cook."

His stomach growled. Seizing the moment, I mentioned she could turn out a meal fit for a king. His stomach growled again.

Grudgingly, Pedro accepted the offer to let us rent his cow and use the money for food. He told us with a loud sigh that it had been a while since a woman had cooked in his kitchen.

I asked him if he was a widower.

He closed his eyes and bowed his head. "*Si*, my beloved Rosa died many years ago."

"Don Pedro," I said. "Do your children live near-by?"

"They used to, but not anymore. I have two boys and a girl. Both my sons are in Texas now. My daughter's husband died on the way there. He paid a Coyote to take him to San Antonio, but he was locked in a hot box trailer with other unfortunate souls. They were abandoned to die in a place called Corpus Christi. Soon after his death, Maria, my daughter, brought her boys to live with me. When they were settled, she left for Chicago to meet with a cousin who had a job in a restaurant. She made it without any problems. Thanks to God almighty. Maria has a good job now, she sends money from time to time, as do my sons. Life here is good for an old man, but it lacks opportunities for the young, especially those with ambition."

He mentioned there was a store close by where supplies could be purchased. He also explained, with some concern, that the cow in the backyard was their only means of daily support. "We get milk from the cow twice a day, and we trade it for things we need. I am not convinced Lucinda can pull your big car, but since you are my guests, I'll go along with your suggestion."

That being decided, the old man fetched his sombrero. Ramona and the three boys headed to the store.

Charlene, Pedro, Junior, and I walked with the cow. I was hoping Lucinda wouldn't die pulling Charlene's heavy car.

We found the Mercury Marquis station wagon where we left it. A rope with a loose knot was placed around the cow's neck. The other end was tied to the bumper of the car. Charlene walked alongside the driver's door. She had the window down and was pushing and steering at the same time. Junior and I pushed from behind. Pedro led and encouraged the unhappy cow, swatting it with a stick.

Halfway there I was beginning to think this affair looked like another one of my hare-brained ideas. The cow was straining so much she was leaking milk. I could tell the old man was worried. I felt bad.

We finally made it to the house, and none too soon either, because the cow looked exhausted. I was relieved and thanked God for his kindness.

Pedro grabbed a bucket, filled it with water from the cistern, and washed Lucinda's udders. Then he poured the rest of the water on the hot cow.

Ramona and the boys returned from the store. With them was a man leading a burro. There was an extra kid with them.

Pedro went outside and greeted the donkey-driver. The beast of burden had two deep wicker baskets attached to a homemade wooden apparatus that was designed to accommodate the baskets, which were full of groceries. We were told the muleskinner was the husband of the woman who ran the store.

"What's with the burro?" I asked Ramona

"Any purchase of twenty-five dollars or more comes with free home delivery. I also bought two gallons of gasoline."

"They had gas at the store?"

"Well, not exactly. There was a man at the store with a truck. He was buying a sack of flour and heard one of Pedro's boys say we'd run out of gas. He charged me five dollars for each gallon he siphoned out of his vehicle. He would have sold me the whole tank, but his wife would only allow him to sell me two."

"I'm willing to bet the house this is the first home delivery that store ever had," I said.

"Probably so, the whole area seems very poor. The lady who owned the store was surprised to see me walk up with the kids. I made her day."

"I bet you did. Her husband also seems impressed."

The owner of the burro couldn't keep his eyes off Ramona's breasts. I couldn't believe she went to the store wearing a low-cut halter-top with no bra, and short-shorts.

The sight of her long curvy slender legs was dangerous enough, throw in a view of those two large delicious puppies into the mix and you had danger written all over her.

Ramona had no sense of modesty. Mom was going to shit-a-brick when she came face to face with her new soon to be daughter-in-law. My future bride loved to wear as little clothing as possible.

All that exposed skin had crumbled my resistance. I was hooked before I thought the whole deal out. I remember the first time I saw her. My eyes nearly popped out of their sockets. It was summer in Houston, and she was cavorting with some friends at Memorial Park. She had on a pair of cut-off jean shorts with a slit on each side, and wore no panties. Her nipples were trying to break out of the thin fabric that tried to pass for a halter top. I didn't have a chance.

I understood the reason for the boy's presence. The woman who ran the store sent him along to make damn sure her husband behaved. Ramona was hot.

To my annoyance, she had purchased two scrawny live chickens. However, my discomfort was eased when I was told the donkey driver was also a chicken killer, and feather-plucker. Ramona was a clever shopper. She came home with food, gas, and a butcher.

Nonetheless, she made the mistake of returning with a month's supply of food, causing Pedro to complain the purchases exceeded the money paid for the cow's services. Furthermore, he insisted that due to the amount of food bought, we had to stay a few days with them to help eat it.

Charlene glared at me when I accepted the offer.

"Don't give me any dirty looks," I said. "Your daughter is to blame. If she hadn't purchased the whole store, we'd be out of here tomorrow."

Ramona overheard me. "I didn't spend all twenty-five dollars on food and gas. I also bought the boys water pistols and yo-yos. You can't believe how cheap things are here."

One hour later there was a commotion in the back yard. I went out to investigate and found Pedro mad as hell. He was collecting the water pistols from the kids. As he passed me, he glared and muttered. "Water pistols are totally unsuited for our household. It causes Antonio and Armando to ignore the rules of water conservation."

"You're having a drought?"

With a scowl on his face, he said, "No, we have a small cistern."

He handed me Raul's gun, and threw the other's into the trash bucket. Then he disappeared into his bedroom.

Pedro didn't stay mad for very long. The aroma of Ramona's cooking had hypnotic powers. He came out with a smile that said volumes about her culinary skills.

I patted him on the back and whispered, "As I said, Don Pedro, you and the boys are in for a special treat. There is a reason why I'm marrying her."

He looked her over. "I can't believe a woman that looks like that can also cook. You are a lucky man, Alex."

We made small talk during dinner and ate to our heart's content. But Ramona had prepared too much food, and there was some left.

Pedro looked at the leftovers with righteous anger. "The main difference between our cultures has to do with the fact you Gringos have too much, and we Mexicans have too little. You cook without regard to how many people are eating. We count heads, and take into consideration the appetite of those sitting at the table. There is never any leftover food."

Charlene was bristling with anger. I was hoping Mata-Hari would control herself, but she didn't. She snarled and defended her way of life. "With all due respect, Don Pedro, the main difference between our cultures has to do with electricity. Everyone in the United States has refrigeration. If we cook too much, we put the leftovers in the fridge. In our culture, especially in Texas, it is considered bad manners to prepare barely enough food to cover the guest's appetites. It is always better to have too much than not enough. Besides, we have dogs to feed."

Pedro became outraged. Charlene's contempt for poverty made him mad. He slammed his fist on the table, knocking the plastic tumblers to the floor.

I braced for an outright brawl. The old hyena was out of booze, and seemed to be in a nasty mood.

Before our host could come up with a reply, Ramona's sharp

sense of awareness kicked into gear. She jumped into the fray and told Pedro there was enough leftover stew to give his skinny dogs a nice meal. Obviously he misunderstood Ramona's comment, because he glared at her.

To my surprise, the expected scuffle didn't materialize. The old guy looked at Ramona, and then at his hungry dogs. He agreed to her suggestion, thanked her for the nice meal, and left the table. He entered his room and closed the door.

While the dishes were being washed, I admonished Charlene for insulting our host. "I can't believe you behaved so badly, you ought to be ashamed."

"Up yours, Alex. Education is everyone's duty. Pedro needed to have a class in Texas culture. Now he knows why we are different. You are nothing but an ass kisser."

After the women cleaned the kitchen, we agreed to bed down early so we could get up at the crack of dawn and help the old man with his chores. We made a pact to accept his hospitality for one more night.

Antonio and Armando were gracious enough to offer Charlene and Ramona their bedroom. It had two cots in it. I took the hammock in the living room. The kids slept outside in our tent.

In the middle of a good dream, I heard a loud "psst." I tried to block the intrusion. I was in the process of removing the panties from a woman. I wanted to see if she was a real blonde, yet the "psst's" kept on coming. Grudgingly, I abandoned the dream, opened one eye, stretched my neck, and noticed Junior. He was standing by the open window.

"Psst, Mister Alex, you better get up, we have a big problem."

I climbed out of the hammock and went outside. "What's the problem, Junior?"

"Look over there, Mister Alex. The cow is dead."

My heart sank. Pedro's cow, his only source of income was lying on the ground all stretched-out and stiff.

"Oh, no, what happened?"

"I don't know. I got up to piss and saw the cow lying on the ground, dead. I think it died of a heart attack. I think making the old cow pull your heavy American car killed her. I think you are in trouble plenty. What do you think?"

Junior was right. I killed the old man's cow. I felt terrible. I had to think and come up with an idea, and fast. "I have a plan," I said.

"Is it as good as the last one? Getting an old cow to pull a heavy car was a stupid idea."

I winced. The ratty kid was poking me again. Needing to get control of the situation, I whispered to the scamp. "Be quiet, Junior, no need to cry over spilled milk. If we can pull this off, there's a ten-spot in it for you. Now, pay attention and let me explain the plan...."

Twenty minutes later I'm sneaking into the boy's bedroom. I placed my hand on Ramona's mouth. She woke up and looked at me with scared eyes. I placed a finger on my lips and slowly removed my hand from her mouth.

"What's going on, Alex?"

"We have a big problem. Wake your mother and meet me outside. Get your gear and be ready to ride."

"What? What's going on?"

"Don't ask any questions. You will know why we have to leave as soon as you come outside. Please wake your mother and get dressed without making any noise. Be quick about it."

"The cow's dead, isn't it?"

My heart dropped. "What made you think of that?"

"Mother told me you talked Pedro into hitching his old cow to the car instead of the young ox. The cow's dead, isn't it?"

Shit, Charlene is going to level dirt on me. I hated to give that dreadful woman reason to abuse me. Hell, I deserved it. The stiff-legged cow in the backyard was damaging testimony.

"Yes, the cow is dead. Get your mother up. We are running away."

In no time at all, and I must admit it, I had never seen Charlene move so quickly before, we were in the car and out of there. I left a note for Pedro, apologizing for the good deed going bad, and attached a hundred dollars to it.

Once we were a distance away, Charlene dove into me. First she yelled at me for getting an old cow to pull a heavy car. Then she scolded me for leaving the brand new tent behind. "Now we don't have one. What are we going to do if we get stranded somewhere?"

"Losing the tent was unfortunate," I said, "but Armando and

Antonio were sleeping inside. Junior was lucky to get Raúl out without waking them up. What was I supposed to do? Wake them up, and then tie and gag them?"

I tried unsuccessfully to defend myself by pleading a momentary lapse of reason, but that didn't work. Then, to increase my level of glumness, Ramona threw fuel onto a roaring fire by telling everyone that I once forgot to tie a piano I was transporting on the back of a pick-up truck. "Alex made a sharp turn and it fell off, breaking into a million pieces."

Charlene's eyes gleamed at the revelation. I felt betrayed.

Junior eyes showed disappointment. "You don't know about ropes, Mister Alex?"

There he goes again, another shot. I kept quiet. I could tell I was losing his reverence. Even though I resented his smug attitude, keeping the ragamuffin's respect seemed important. I couldn't give him the top spot.

We drove for a while in silence. We left the forest and passed through an area with acres and acres of sugar cane fields. The women and Raúl slept in the back seat. Junior was sleeping in the front.

I glanced down, checked the gas gauge and became worried. San Cristobal De Las Casas was still a good fifty miles away, and the Mercury was good for about sixteen miles to the gallon. I was going to run out of gas, again.

Junior must have sensed my discomfort because he woke up. He bummed a cigarette and asked me in Spanish, so the women would not understand, if I really forgot to tie the piano.

"Look," I said. "I did it on purpose. I was bringing home a piano for Ramona, and she's a terrible player. She was going to drive me crazy playing the damn thing, so I dropped it by accident, on purpose."

Junior looked at me for a minute, trying to digest my statement. Then, a smile slowly appeared. "You're a smart man, Mister Alex. What a good way of not coming home with the piano."

Soon we were smoking and bonding. *So what if I lied to him. One lie always deserves another.* Between us, it was difficult to tell which one was the biggest liar. He was no more the son of Jimmy Buffet than I was.

I looked at the gas gauge again and began to sweat. Junior

followed my eyes and noticed the dilemma. "What are you going to do about that?" he said, pointing at the gauge.

"I'm not sure, but when I think of something you'll be the first to know."

A few miles further there was a car parked on the side of the road. I stopped behind it and climbed out.

Ramona woke up. "What's wrong, Alex?"

"We're almost out of gas. I'm going to try and buy some from the person that owns that car."

She stretched, mentioned she needed to see a-man-about-a-horse, grabbed the toilet paper roll and left the car. I often wondered what that saying had to do with taking a dump. It didn't make any sense.

Charlene was still asleep, so was Raúl. I counted my blessings, no need for the old grizzly to show her teeth. I grabbed the empty five-gallon gas container and went to find the driver. Junior left in the direction of Ramona.

I looked inside the car and saw a man sleeping. I woke him up, negotiated a deal for some gas and he siphoned five-gallons out of his tank. I put it in the Mercury.

When I was done, I went to see what was keeping Ramona. I made a turn through a gap of mesquite trees, and spotted Junior. He was crouching behind a bush having sex with himself. I looked again and saw the reason. He was peeping at Ramona. She had removed her pants and was washing herself in a creek. I picked up a rock and threw it at him.

He looked at me and took off running. I gave chase. He stumbled, and I caught him. I grabbed the squirming kid by the arm and thumped him on the head with my knuckles.

"I'm sorry, Mister Alex," he pleaded. "Please don't give me another coscorrón, they hurt."

"You were whacking off while spying on Ramona, you little twerp. I have a mind to tell her."

"Please, Mister Alex, don't say nothing to her. I couldn't help myself. I went out to piss, and then I saw her take her pants off. When she began to wash her bush I lost control. I am a man, I have needs."

"You're a dirty kid. You shouldn't be doing that."

"Don't you play with yourself?"

20

"Yes, sometimes."

"I do it sometimes too, especially when confronted with such a sight. You're a lucky man, Mister Alex."

I grabbed him by the neck of his shirt and walked him back to the car.

Charlene was awake and talking to the man that sold me the gas. I wondered if she realized the guy didn't speak English. Raúl was urinating on the man's car tire.

Ramona finally returned. Junior gave me a pleading look. "Please Mister Alex, don't tell her nothing."

Oh, what the hell. I handled myself plenty while looking at naked girls in magazines. Junior's action was understandable. Ramona's physical attributes were indeed tantalizing. I let go of the shirt and patted him on the back.

"Don't do it again," I said.

Finally, all was well, and we were on the road again. Feeling complacent, I told them that I was surprised the man sold me five gallons worth. I figured since San Cristobal was at least fifty miles away, he would only give up one, or maybe two gallons.

"How much did he charge you?" Charlene asked.

"I got a better deal than Ramona. I offered him three dollars per gallon. We can't be spending money like drunken sailors. That cow ordeal cost me a hundred dollars."

"You gave that old man a hundred dollars for a two-hundred dollar cow?" Charlene said. "What a cheapskate you are. It's a good thing I left him a hundred dollars under my pillow."

"You left him a hundred dollars for a two hundred dollar cow? What a cheapskate you are," I said.

"I didn't kill the damn cow."

"I left him two hundred dollars under my pillow," Ramona said.

"Mama Mia!" bellowed Junior. "Let me see if I can understand this. You guys gave the old man four hundred dollars for a hundred dollar cow?"

Before he could say another word, I made a curve and there was a PEMEX gas station. I felt hustled.

"That man knew very well there was a gas station here and didn't tell me," I said, feeling the fool.

"Let me see if I understand this," repeated Junior. "You paid

21

three dollars a gallon for gasoline that cost only ninety cents a gallon?"

Christ, he's at it again. "How was I supposed to know the station was around the corner? I am a damn tourist. I don't know the lay of the land."

"Okay," Junior said. "If you guys want to make it to San Cristobal with money, you need a business manager. I'm not a tourist, but a Mexican kid with a good idea of where things are, what they cost, and how they work. I'm applying for the job."

"How much will it cost us?" asked Ramona.

"I can't believe you're considering it. I am more than capable of handling things."

Sensing an opportunity to humiliate me, Charlene agreed we would be better off with Junior in charge, but she demanded to know how much his services were going to cost.

"Five dollars a day," he said.

"Good," Charlene said. "Alex will pay you."

"What? Five dollars a day is highway robbery. You're no better than the guy who sold me the gas."

"Mister Alex, please listen to me. For five dollars a day, I will keep you from buying cows, expensive gas, and getting into trouble with the police. Besides, with a job I can pay for my and Raúl's way. I can give you five dollars a day for our expenses."

I couldn't believe it. The rascal was offering me my own money back. I needed to be careful. This kid was good.

Ramona smiled and put her arm around his neck and said, "All in favor of hiring Junior to be our business road manager, please say aye."

Charlene, Ramona, and Junior said "aye." Raúl raised his hand.

"How come Raúl raised his hand?" I asked. "I thought he didn't understand English."

"Just because he doesn't have words, doesn't mean he don't know what's going on. He's mute not stupid."

Charlene and Ramona had a good laugh. Junior smiled, and Raúl crawled unto Ramona's lap. Feeling like a fool, I kept quiet and bit my lip.

Soon everyone was asleep again. I drove, trying to think of ways to get revenge. *No way am I going to allow a ratty kid to get the best of me.* I turned a corner, and in front of me was a police roadblock. I stopped, there were several cars ahead of me. I looked through the rear view mirror at all the new electrical merchandise we had in the back of the station wagon and grimaced. The bribe to cross was going to be expensive. I swallowed my pride, and woke the imp.

"Hey Junior...."

This story was part of an unfinished novel. To test the strength of the manuscript, Arcia entered the piece into a chapter contest sponsored by an accomplished English writer from Derbyshire, named Neal James. First prize was a month-long promotion of the book in East Midlands, England. It won, and Arcia had thirty days to hand over the novel so it could be promoted. He finished the manuscript, had it edited, published, and into Neal's hands before time expired. "In Search of High Ground" - The Amorous Antics of Alex Perez is Arcia's second novel. It's also his most imaginative works, and displays his penchant for mixing slapstick, with dry, murky humor. Rated PG

A Park Bench & Cigarettes

I found myself riding in a bus, staring out the window at a dark countryside. The ride had an eerie feel to it; my fellow passengers were faceless. When I couldn't feel the road beneath my feet, panic set in. *Where am I?*

Soon there were lights glowing on the horizon. The bus entered a city and came to a stop at a station. I got off, walked outside, and asked a porter where I was.

He smiled at me and removed his sombrero. "Mister, you are in Puerto Vallarta. *Bienvenido.* Can I carry your luggage?"

How in hell did I get to Mexico? I checked my pant and shirt pockets for a baggage ticket, but couldn't find any. There was none in my wallet either. Obviously I didn't check any.

"No tengo maletas," I said to him.

As soon as he understood I had no baggage and wasn't going to need a porter, he moved on to the next guy.

I looked in my wallet again, and counted the bills. Ninety-five bucks. *Shit, I'm broke.* I walked to the street corner and flagged a cab. Since I didn't have a hotel reservation, I asked the cabbie if he knew of an inexpensive place close to the water. He zoomed through stop signs and red lights, dropping me off at El Hotel Coronado.

I looked at the seedy building and rolled my eyes. Hell, I deserved it. I asked to be taken to a cheap place. This shabby hotel certainly looked affordable. I paid the cabbie three dollars, walked inside the hotel and caught the man behind the counter stuffing his face. He placed his plate of food down and began to pick his teeth with his finger.

Keeping in line with my financial state, I chose to book a room without air-conditioning. They were cheaper, and I intended to sleep with the windows opened anyway.

The man asked for twenty-five dollars. I paid him and he gave me a key, but he shot me a disapproving look when he realized I had no luggage.

I walked up two sets of stairs, found my room, opened the door and hit the light switch. A lamp came on. I grimaced as two cockroaches ran down a wall. Other than the unwelcomed insects and a faint smell of sanitizer, the room had a pleasant rustic ambiance.

The brown and green colors of the printed coconut trees on the off-white wallpaper were badly faded, and doubling down at the corners. The bed was hard, and the mirror on the credenza had a crack running through the middle. The chest of drawers had no knobs. Big whoop. I didn't care. However, I howled when I realized the room came without an indoor toilet.

I stared with disbelief at the sign that stated the bathroom was outside, at the end of the corridor. What the hell, I can always piss out a window.

Looking out one of them, I saw businesses packed into a dimly lit street called Cortez. From the other window I saw a park illuminated by a full moon. If I stretched my neck, I could see a sliver of the Pacific Ocean.

I continued to scan the area and noticed a place called Pizzeria Pisano. By the size of the crowd crammed into the courtyard, the food had to be good. I made a mental note to eat there, but first my body demanded rest. I was tired and wanted to lay down.

I had barely stretched my aching body on the bed when a sudden burst of wind, accompanied by rain forced me to get up and close the windows. That killed any chances of getting a good night's sleep. Upset, I vacated my hot room, found the bathroom, walked down the stairs, and went out in the rain searching for an all-night bar.

A few beers and a half-dozen tequila shots later, I stumbled out of the bar and headed towards the park. I needed to contemplate my situation. I was lucky to find an empty bench, as most were being used as beds. I sat, lit my last American cigarette, and began to think and blow smoke circles into the air.

There was an old woman sweeping the sidewalk with a big straw broom. She had a bedraggled appearance and seemed to be sharing a laugh with someone sitting on a bench. Upon closer inspection, the man she was chatting with was sleeping.

The old hag reminded me of a song by the Mexican rock

group, *Mana*. It was called *"El Muelle de San Blas."* The song told the story of an old mad woman who had spent her life hanging out at a dock in Puerto Vallarta waiting for a lover who had left on a ship, promising to return, but never did.

When I tried to trace the steps that brought me here, all I got was a murky picture of a wasted life. I wasn't sure how or why I came here, but I can tell you Puerto Vallarta felt like the end of the line. Hell, I couldn't even explain why I was in Mexico. Last recollection had me in France. I guess the drunken binge had been long and strenuous. Nothing kills your short-term memory better than a heavy dose of booze.

I kept my eyes on the old woman as she swept the garbage-strewn sidewalk. By the amount of it, there must have been a lot of late night revelers. At times she would cackle and slap her knee. She seemed to be enjoying a singular conversation. *She's probably crazy as a loon.* I wondered how long it would take for misery to overpower reality, and force me into her world.

Absurdity aside, the scraggly old woman seemed contented. *Hell, she was probably better off than me.* Her world had to be friendlier, probably a place void of emotional stress. A world where oblivion ruled, and the heart ceased to be nothing more than a mechanical component. I felt listless. I'd been abandoned by zeal and laughter. They had gone on an extended holiday. My life was shit.

I decided to get a grip, no need to wallow in self-pity. After all, I was in Mexico, not in Albania. I should try and make the best out of the situation.

The park reminded me of Panama. There were tall palm trees all over the place. It also had a short seawall, affording me a good view of the water from the bench. The beauty of the palms added to the ambiance of the area. Frankly, the feel of this place soothed my sense of romanticism.

I tried to comprehend the reason why I was in Puerto Vallarta. Something radical must have happened to bring me here. *But what?*

The sun began to light up the park. Soon the area started coming to life. I scanned the emerging crowd. Peddlers were out selling everything from tortillas to newspapers. A policeman began to run off the bums and drunks who had taken possession of the park benches. Before long, the place was teeming with activity. Yet there was an oddity that caught my eye. The expressions on the people were grim. Not a single soul in the crowd was smiling.

It was then, when I was scanning the faces that I saw her. She was standing next to a palm tree gazing toward the horizon. She was wearing a soiled white dress, and her coiffed hair was beginning to unravel. If you stretched the imagination you could say she looked dressed for a wedding. I felt a bond between us. Here was a kindred soul. Maybe life had betrayed her as well. Two lost souls brought together by the whims of fate; how poignantly romantic.

To my embarrassment, she turned and glued her eyes on mine. They looked cold. Her expression gave me the impression she was reading my mind. I swallowed hard, feeling guilty at being caught invading her privacy. I scanned her countenance and noticed a posture that clearly told me to mind my own damn business. *Who in hell did she think she was? I'm allowed my own thoughts.* Resentful of her resentfulness, I continued with my mental intrusion.

The idea of approaching her, and trying my luck did cross my mind. After all, she was an attractive woman in an odd sort of way. Yet her stance was hostile and certainly uninviting. In the end, I decided it was best to keep my distance, no need to lose my seat on the bench.

The old hag kept on sweeping the cracked cement sidewalk. She finally made it to my bench, and caught me looking at her. She scowled, and spat on the pavement.

"*Que estás viendo, pendejo?*"

"I'm looking at your ugly face, old woman. You have a problem with that?"

"You want to look at something ugly, you stupid *gringo*? Then you take a good look at this!" She turned around, bent over, pulled her skirt up to her waist, and showed me sagging bare buttocks.

"Aught! Stop that, you are burning my eyes. Get out of here! You are nothing but a dirty old wench. Be off before I call the police."

She cackled, slapped her knee, and walked away.

The woman in the white dress laughed. I figured she would come over, but she didn't. A few minutes later she opened her purse and pulled out a pack of cigarettes. She fumbled for one, but didn't find any. She looked at me, crushed her pack, threw it on the ground, and came over to my bench. She walked towards me with a heavy pace, and without any hip movement.

When she came closer, I noticed a pale face with a pair of blood-shot eyes imbedded inside dark circles.

"Mister, do you have a cigarette?"

I showed her my empty pack. She placed her hands on her waist and frowned. "Do you mind if I sit by you, *gringo*?"

"I'm not a *gringo*, but yes, you can sit down."

"You look like one."

"Story of my life, but I'm fine with it. Do you want me to be one?"

She forced a smile, but remained quiet. Feeling good about her response to my effort at civility, I decided to pry into her life.

"The dress you are wearing could pass for a wedding dress, did you...?"

"Vete al diablo, cabron!" she yelled, and walked off to retake her place by the palm tree.

I couldn't believe she called me a bastard and told me to go to hell. *What's the deal with these people?* Everyone seems to be hostile. *I was right. She has been jilted.* Now, how do I, other than by using a common apologetic gesture repair the damage?

I worked out a strategy and stood up, but when I began to walk her way, a man wearing an oversized trench coat and baseball cap, standing about ten yards away made a move towards my bench. *No way, mister, you're not getting my bench.* I sat back down.

He glared at me and spat on the pavement.

I placed my hand on the side of my face, and casually shot him the bird.

He stared at me for a few seconds, then started to walk my way.

Oh, shit, now what? I hope he's not going to hit me.

The man came over. He stood and stared at me.

I gave him a nervous smile. He didn't respond with one of his own. Instead, he stood there looking at me in total silence. I was about to say something when he opened his coat and showed me his sagging belly, hairy balls, and a limp dick.

"Aught! Get out of here, you pervert! Go flash little girls."

The man smiled, closed his coat, removed his cap, bowed

gracefully and walked away. The woman in the white dress laughed again. I tipped my Fedora to her, she acknowledge my courtesy and came over.

"*Oye, gringo*, can I sit with you without getting insulted?"

"Yes, of course. My quota of insults has been filled. The flasher singed my eyebrows."

She looked at me with languid eyes. "You have a cigarette?"

I showed her the empty packet. "Sorry, I'm still out of smokes."

She sighed, shrugged her shoulders and slumped on the bench. "It's okay, mister, you don't have to be sorry. I'm just short on luck these days."

"Aren't we all? What's your story?"

She gave me a sad smile, and then grabbed her dress. "My boyfriend left me standing at the altar with my parents watching."

I gave her an apologetic smile, then touched her hand. It was cold. We sat next to each other for a while without speaking. I scanned her facial features. She had high cheekbones, brownish-red hair coming to a widow's peak. Her blood-shot eyes were brown, and her face had more lines than I had discerned. I tried to guess her age. She was probably in her thirties. She stretched her legs and looked down, rubbing a protruding belly. I saw dried blood, and a cut on her wrist.

"I have made three big mistakes in my life," she said, "and all three involved the same man."

After that unwanted revelation, I needed a cigarette. "Would you mind saving my seat on this bench? I will go and get two packs of smokes, one for you. Maybe I'll score us a few tacos, and a couple of beers."

"*Seguro,*" she said. "I'll wait for you."

I stood up and headed out. Thirty feet from the street I looked back, and to my horror, she had gotten up and was leaving the bench. I saw a thug point to it and grab a hold of a woman's hand. I dashed back and sat on it. He was not amused by my speedy return.

"*Qué carajo haces aquí, gringo. Quien te dijo que esta banca es tuya?*"

"My reason for being here is none of your business," I said. "And no, I do not own the bench, but it's mine as long as I'm sitting on it. You need to move on and find another one."

He grabbed me by the shirt and pulled me off the bench. He was about to pound me when the policeman that had been running the bums off the benches blew his whistle.

The lawman came over and had a discussion with the thug. The man cursed me, and walked away with his girlfriend in tow.

"I'm sorry, Mister *Gringo*, these *pachucos* think they own the street. I hope you are not hurt."

"I'm not a *gringo*, but I'm fine, thank you."

"You look like one to me."

"Listen, to you, anyone with white skin and green eyes is a *gringo*."

"No, mister, you are wrong. I know a *gringo* when I see one, and I'm looking at one this very minute."

"I beg to differ."

"You don't have to beg for nothing, just give me five dollars and you can sit on this bench all day. For seven dollars you can sleep on it tonight."

I looked at the policeman. His uniform fit him like a zoot suit. Being short of money, and galled at his brazen attempt at picking my pocket, I went on the offensive.

"I slept here last night, and didn't have to pay you any money."

"You are a liar, *gringo*, everyone who was here last night got picked up by the *diablitos*. The boat came to get them. No one escapes them, they know who you are."

"That may be so, but I'm here to tell you I came to the park late last night and didn't see you, so I'm not paying a cent."

"You are a damned liar, *gringo*. You came here early this morning, that's why I didn't see you last night. You, the woman in the bridal dress, the *pachuco* and his girlfriend, and the man with the overcoat, all of you came to the park this morning. You will be gone by midnight."

"Gone where?"

"You don't even know why you are here, do you? You better stay close to your bench, there are bound to be more like you coming today."

"I'm not paying you any money to sit on this bench, this is a public park. Be off with you before I call the police."

"I am the *pinche* police, you stupid *Americano*, pay me or leave."

Tiring of the foolishness, I gave the policeman five dollars. He tucked the money in his pocket and left laughing. I sat back down and tried to make sense out of the conversation. *What does he mean I'll be gone by midnight?* What does he mean the devils will pick me up?

I looked to my left and saw the woman in the white dress walking my way. *Oh, God, not her again.* To my right, the cop was jostling another unfortunate soul out of money.

The need to curse the woman for breaking her promise was strong. Yet as she came closer, I changed my mind. She seemed tired and irritated. It was prudent to stay quiet. Maybe she would go away.

"Hola, gringo, you have any cigarettes?"

Oh, God, this is ridiculous. Hell, two can play this game. "Sure, let me give you one." I took out my pack and handed it to her.

She fumbled with it, found it to be empty, crushed it, threw it on the ground and glared at me. "This is the same pack you had before, what is wrong with you?"

"Nothing is wrong with me, but I'm beginning to suspect that there might be something wrong with you."

"You are going to insult me again?"

"No, no insult intended. It's just that I asked you to wait here while I went to buy us cigarettes. As soon as I left, you did too."

"So, what's the big deal with this bench anyway? You attached at the hip to it? Tell me the truth gringo, are you weird or something?"

"No, I'm not peculiar, but I do want to keep my seat on this bench. My buttocks, not my hips have become attached to it. They enjoy sitting on it. Do you want a cigarette or not?"

"Yes, why do you think I'm here for?"

I rolled my eyes and pondered the situation out loud. "How can I get you a cigarette, and at the same time keep my seat on this bench? You have any ideas?"

She gave me a cold stare. "You are stupider than you look. Listen, I can wait here until you return, or you can glue your skinny ass to the bench and give me some money. I will go get us cigarettes."

I thought about giving her the money, but I wasn't sure she would return with the smokes and my change. "If I go get the cigarettes, would you stay here and guard the bench?"

"Guard it from what? Do you think we have bench stealers here? The thing is stuck to the ground with cement."

I was about to pull my hair when I decided to try a new approach. "What is your name?" I said.

"Why do you want to know?"

"It would be nice to address you by your proper name."

"First you insult me, and now you want to be nice? I don't know if I want to give you my name."

"Okay, fine, we can keep this clinical if you like."

She looked at me with wide eyes, and moved away from me. "What do you mean by clinical? Are you sick or something?"

"No, I'm not sick, but you probably are."

"There you go again, more insults. What is your problem?"

"I don't have a problem."

As soon as that ridiculous statement left my mouth, I cringed.

"Okay, let's be fair here. I will admit to having more than my share of problems, but you are not helping me here. Do you want a cigarette or not?"

"Of course. Why do you think I'm here for?"

I clenched my fists, gritted my teeth, and stood up. "If I leave to get us two packs of cigarettes, will you stay here and not go anywhere?"

"Of course I will. Bring me back a taco and a cold beer too."

I bit my lip, left the bench, and crossed the street. I told myself not to look back, but ventured a look anyway. As was the norm, the woman was not there. I scanned the area and saw an American soldier walking towards the bench. I panicked and tried to run across the street, but the traffic slowed me down and the soldier beat me to it. Anxiety took over. The military man had taken control of the bench. Yet, all was not lost. He had made one big mistake. He was sitting on one side. I rushed and sat on the other side.

The soldier gave me a rueful look, which I acknowledge with one of my own. A few minutes later, I glanced his way and noticed a large bloodied spot on his shirt.

33

"Are you all right?" I said.

"Yes, for the most part I am. Thank you for asking."

"What happened to you?"

He looked at me strangely. "What do you mean what happened to me?"

Good grief, is everyone in this park mental? "Your shirt, it is covered in blood. How did it happen? You get mugged by *pachucos?"*

He looked at his shirt, then at me. "Don't rightly know. Maybe I've been in a fight. It's probably a knife wound. Don't concern yourself with it. It doesn't hurt."

"What's an American soldier doing in Mexico?"

He looked at me with lifeless eyes and ignored my question. Then he turned his back to me.

Okay, two can play the same game. I turned also, but to my vexation, in my line of vision was the woman in the white dress. She was heading my way. *Oh, no, not her again.*

She saw me, came over and sat between the soldier and me. *"Oye, gringo,* did you get any cigarettes?"

Not wanting to get involved in a ludicrous conversation, I kept the answer short and simple. "No, I didn't, I'm sorry."

"But you went to get them. I saw you cross the street. What happened?"

"I never made it to the store. Sorry."

She gave me the bad-eye while mumbling something unintelligible. Then she turned her attention to the soldier.

"Oye, soldado, you got any cigarettes?"

"No, ma'am, I don't smoke. But if I did, I would gladly give you one."

"See, this gringo soldier, he is nice. You are nothing but a *pendejo."*

"Calling me an asshole is not going to get you any smokes. You need to try a different approach."

"So, you think I'm going to blow you for a cigarette, is that it? Just because you are a handsome man you think I'm going to degrade myself? No way, I don't need one that bad."

She turned her attention back to the soldier. "What do you think of a man that wants a blow job for a cigarette?"

I turned beet red. Before I could contradict her statement, the

34

soldier grabbed me by the shirt collar and pulled me towards him.

"You need to apologize to the lady and give her a damn cigarette. You are a sorry excuse for an American."

"Actually, I'm not an American, so there! Also, I don't want a blow job from this crazy woman. And, if it's any of your business, which it isn't, it is a well-known fact, especially to most of us sitting on this park bench that I don't have any cigarettes. But if it pleases your American sense of etiquette, I will give you some money, and you can go and buy us cigarettes. What do you say, soldier boy? Will you get us a couple packs of smokes? I have a twenty dollar bill."

"What do you think I am, mister, a pauper? I don't need your stinking money. I'll go get the woman a pack of smokes."

He let go of my shirt and turned towards her. "Do you like any particular brand, ma'am?"

She looked at me. "What kind do you smoke?"

"I smoke all kinds, but I prefer Marlboros."

"Get me some Vice Roy's," she said.

The soldier got up and left.

"What was the purpose in asking me what I liked, if you were going to order what you wanted all along? I'm not amused."

"Don't be getting all *macho* with me, *gringo*. You told me you smoked all kinds, so I ordered what I liked. You don't like Vice Roy's?"

"I haven't tasted a Vice Roy since I was a kid, and I didn't like them then."

"Well maybe you will like them today. If not, you can go screw yourself."

A short while later, she stood up and started to walk away.

"Hey, where are you going?" I said. "Don't you want to wait for the soldier to return with your cigarettes?"

"No, you wait and keep them for me. Your ass can't seem to leave the bench. I will come back later."

Two hours passed and I was still waiting. The soldier never came back, and neither did the woman in the white dress. Needing a smoke and not wanting to lose my seat on the bench, I allowed my anxiety to kick into a higher gear. To my distress, there wasn't a single vendor within sight. It became apparent that I was going to have to vacate the bench.

I took a deep breath and checked the perimeters. *What luck, there's no one in sight.* The plan was to run and buy cigarettes, book another night at the hotel, and then come back and reclaim the bench. Feeling good about the decision, I left the park bench, found a store and bought two packs of smokes.

The front desk clerk in my hotel was stuffing himself again. He saw me looking at his food and stopped eating. He placed his fork down, and wiped his mouth with a white cloth.

"*Gringo*, what do you want?"

"I'm here to book another night."

"Sorry, we have no more rooms."

"What do you mean you have no room? I didn't check-out."

"You only paid for one night. Your time was up at ten this morning. You didn't bring any clothes with you, and you didn't sleep in your bed, so I figured you were gone. Your room is rented, and we don't have any more. Sorry."

Pissed, I hurried to see if my bench was vacant, it was. Overjoyed, I took a seat in the middle, stretching my arms so no one would have room to squeeze in with me.

Feeling a bit tired, I brought the brim of my Fedora down to keep the sun at bay. It was time for a nap. No sooner had I fallen asleep, than I felt arms shaking my body.

Oh, no, the cop is back. What now? Yet, this action was not followed by the sound of a man's voice, it was an unfamiliar woman's voice.

"Wake up, Monsieur Perez. I am Nurse Miriam Lemieux. I have to change your bandages."

After vigorously objecting (during a fund raising meeting) about the method being used to fund a New Year's Eve party, Arcia was dismissed from the Men's Club of his church by the priest. Instead of throwing a rock through the rectory's window, he decided to write this piece and hopefully get it published in the community newspaper. He wanted to lambast a group of parishioners who followed orders without questioning them. He also wanted to poke a priest who seemed to be out of touch with the financial state of his congregation, and to bash the greed of the Catholic Church. The story never made it into print. Rated PG

The Bishop and the Friars

"The eighth chair belongs to France!" I shouted to Friar John Sebastian.

"What are you talking about, Rodrigo?"

"Sister Marguerite is sitting on a chair which is floating inside the cathedral, and she is telling anyone willing to listen that the eighth chair belongs to France."

"You don't say?"

"I do say, and regrettably so. Would you like to come and see her?"

He agreed, and the race was on….

John Sebastian, being a sprinter in his younger days knew all there was to know about competitive running. He elbowed his way past me as we made a quick turn into the corridor, and then sprinted down the first flight of stairs. He was picking up momentum when he cleared the second set. I could tell he was full of anticipation, he had left me far behind.

Brother John slowed his pace as he made the final turn at the end of the corridor, allowing me to catch up. Cautiously, we approached a mounting and murmuring crowd.

"By God, Rodrigo. You are right!" he exclaimed, as he saw Sister Marguerite floating in the air. "How do you suppose she does that? And, can you tell me why she thinks the eight chair belongs to France? Why not the fourth? Or the sixth?"

"Beats me," I replied. "Maybe it's a hormonal thing."

"Sister Marguerite!" yelled Brother John, causing an echo in the great-hall of the church. "What are you doing up there? Come back down this instant!"

"The eighth chair belongs to France!" She repeated in a loud and defiant voice.

Friar John Sebastian looked at me while scratching his cheek. "What do chairs have to do with France?"

"Who knows?" I said, trying to suppress a smile. "She's a nun; trying to figure them out is a complicated matter."

"Have you checked to see if she has been in the wine cellar,

Rodrigo?"

"What's that got to do with anything?" I said, annoyed at the suggestion. "She is floating on thin air. And, if you look at the long table we set up for the 'Last Supper' scene of our annual program, the eighth chair is gone."

"Oh no," moaned Brother John, "that's Jesus chair. Do you suppose she thinks our lord, Jesus Christ was a Frenchman?"

"Could be, you know how high-minded they are. Yet, if our eyes do not deceive us, Sister Marguerite is suspended in the air. There is a display of power here."

"Oh great," mumbled John Sebastian. "That's all we need now. It's barely two hours before Bishop Graham Owens is scheduled to arrive, and now we are faced with a theological nightmare."

He looked around making sure no one could hear him. "Rodrigo, what are we to do about this? The bishop will open our program, and he will notice Jesus standing up."

"Beats me," I said. "He's from Canada. They have experience dealing with the French. We don't."

"Yes, you are right, Rodrigo. The Canucks do. Boy, that's a bit of luck," he said with a sigh of relief.

Time passed. The crowd grew, and Sister Marguerite kept on shouting that the eight chair belonged to France.

After failing to talk her down, Brother John began to display a troubled countenance. He was clearly worried about the insinuation.

"Rodrigo," he said. "Jesus couldn't have been a Frenchman, could he? Everyone knows he was a Jew."

"Enjoying this unusual situation very much, I went to the cellar and brought up a bottle of ecclesiastical wine and two goblets. I poured us a cup each, and decided to throw fuel into the fire.

"John, you do know that Rabbi Gerard Attia is a Frenchman. "Do you suppose..."

"Don't even say it, Rodrigo. I don't want to deal with such a dilemma. The repercussions would be too dramatic. Jesus has to be a regular Israeli Jew. He couldn't possibly be a French Jew."

"There was no Israel when he was walking on water, remember? Jesus was born in Bethlehem. I do believe he was a

Palestinian Hebrew."

"Shssh!" said Brother John, looking around. "There are Americans in here. They won't put money in the alms basket if you promote the Arab connection."

Bishop Owens arrived and entered the cathedral. It didn't take him long to notice the commotion. He pushed his way through the multitude of people that had gathered inside and were muttering out loud. He burst into the scene, yelling, "What is going on here! Get out the lot of you! This is a house of God, not a market place! Get out! Get out!"

I, Friar Rodrigo Balboa, being blessed with a watchful eye and a keen sense of humor, upon seeing his eminence walk into the cathedral hurried to his side and told him the story.

"So," he said to me, with his chest all puffed up. "She thinks Jesus was a Frenchman, eh? It's typical of them, always giving themselves credit for things not of their doing. Well, stand aside and let me deal with this."

Bishop Owens approached the flying nun and yelled, "Sister Marguerite, you come down this instant!"

"The eighth chair belongs to France!" she repeated with defiance.

"No, it does not!" yelled the bishop. "It's the fifth one. Saint John's chair is the one that belongs to France! His mother was a Frenchwoman. I can't believe you didn't know that!"

"What?" said Sister Marguerite, expressing for the first time doubt in her belief.

"It's the fifth chair, you dimwitted female. That's the one that belongs to France. You are sitting on the wrong one!"

Sister Marguerite began to show visible signs of confusion. She developed a worried expression, and then uttered words that brought forth her demise. "Oh, no! Are you sure?"

That statement, once made betrayed her faith and shattered her resolve, bringing the chair crashing down unto the marble floor with the sound of thunder.

"See," said a cheerful Graham Owens. "That's the reason why I'm the bishop. There is not a problem, theological or otherwise that I cannot resolve, eh."

Then, with pride in his face, he pushed me aside and

approached poor Brother John who was horrified at the injuries sustained by Sister Marguerite.

"Well John, how many tickets did you sell for today's performance?"

Friar John Sebastian, being the man he was, at first could not believe the bishop's words. But his eyes soon cleared, and he mumbled, "Not enough."

He looked around, perplexed. "There was a large crowd here a minute ago. I was hoping to sell them the rest of the tickets. Where did they go?"

In a flash, Bishop Owens was out the cathedral doors yelling, "Wait a minute! Don't go! Come back. We still have tickets available for today's performance!"

"Why did the crowd leave?" asked a distraught John Sebastian.

"Bishop Owens ran them off," I said, proudly. "It had something to do with this being a house of God, not a common marketplace."

"You don't say?"

"I do say," I replied smugly. "And now, at this very moment, he is out in the street trying to sell them the remaining tickets."

"To the same people he ran off?"

"Yes, I'm afraid so," I said, chuckling.

"Does he have the tickets?"

"No," I said, with another chuckle. "We have them in our pockets."

"How can he sell something he doesn't have?"

"Who knows? Maybe bishops can do that."

We looked at each other, and then at Sister Marguerite, who was laying on the marble floor, bloodied, and with visible broken bones.

"What do you think we ought to do about her?" I said to Brother John.

"We ought to help her," he said. "That's a ghastly injury she has on her leg."

"Yes, we could do that," I said. "Or we could leave her for someone else to attend. Then we can go outside and give the bishop the remaining tickets for today's performance. I bet he can sell them all."

We looked at each other, and the race was on....

Written to pay homage to the Fifties – To Panama – To the Canal Zone, and to the end of American colonialism, a grandiose era. Rated G

The Last Mango on the Limb

(To Margaret)

When I was a child, I lived in a place we called paradise. It had another name, but for us it was indeed a place of wonderment.

In the old days it was an island called Manzanillo. Then one day the *gringos* came and started to dig a canal. They removed the dirt and rock from the 'big ditch' and dropped it between the mainland and the island, thus uniting it and creating a de facto peninsula.

We lived there, and so did they. The town was divided into two areas. One for us called Colon, and one for them called Cristobal. As kids we intermingled, played games, and enjoyed the differences that existed between us. We taught them soccer, they taught us American football. We showed them how to play war with fighting tops as well as kites, and play a team running game called *Ringaliyo*. They in turn introduced us to the world of hopscotch, baseball, hide-and-seek, one, two, three, red light, kick the can, and jump rope to a cadence of special songs.

We spent our childhood enjoying each other's company without regard to the fact we were in essence, culturally different.

They spoke English and we spoke Spanish, but we managed to communicate. We, on the Panamanian side were aware of those differences very early in our lives, but enjoyed them nonetheless.

It was the fifties, and a fine time to be alive. Rock and Roll was beginning to consume our attention, as were the gringo girls with their tight blouses and short-shorts. We couldn't help but notice with excitement that their skirts were higher off the ankle. They also wore make-up, and emblazoned their lips with bright red lipstick.

We used to get out of school and run to the park on Seventh Street, which was the border between both cultures in those days. This park had a cement sidewalk with benches about every ten feet on each side. No man's land was the area in the

45

middle, which was void of grass but had huge shade trees. For the most part, we stayed on our side and they kept to theirs, yet we acknowledge each other's presence.

After going home, doing our homework and whatever chores were demanded from our parents, we came out to play by our end of the park. Colon City in the fifties was a nice place for a boy to grow up.

My family owned an icebox, a reel-to reel tape-recorder, a good radio, and a record player. There was a black man that came by our house every morning pushing a heavy wooden handcart selling block ice for these boxes that barely kept our food cool. He would return in the afternoon singing calypso songs and selling refreshingly cold *pipas*, which is a local name for coconuts. Rum and coconut water made a delicious drink.

We had a telephone and the operators knew our family. So, when you made a call, more often than not you had a quick chitchat with the operator before you gave her the number you wanted. However, there was a downside to that friendliness, we had to learn to speak Pig Latin in order to keep our personal business from the eavesdropping operators. In spite of that, life was simple and enjoyable.

In the early fifties a nickel bought you a soda, a sweet roll, or a single scoop ice cream cone. A movie ticket cost a dime for the early Saturday morning matinee. For twenty-five cents you could see a feature Hollywood movie. A Mexican film cost fifteen cents.

Going to the movies was not only special it was a family occasion. After church, on Sunday, we went to grandmother's house for lunch. Then we were off to the movies.

In the early stages of my life, the family attended the same theater. Then, as we grew up, we went to different ones. I still remember the excitement that encircled the whole family as we rode in dad's 1948 Dodge Coupe to the movies. At the beginning, there was the annoying newsreel. That was followed by previews of coming attractions. Next came a short film, usually the Three Stooges. The cartoon came before the main attraction started.

Everything had to be done in a specific order. Dad had to be in his seat before the newsreel started. Mom didn't care when

46

we arrived, as long as it was before the main attraction, and us kids were focused on the short film, and cartoon.

We always came early, purchased the tickets, bought cold *chichas*, and either won tons, or popcorn soaked in butter.

Somewhere along the way, the corruption of modernization began to affect us. First our lives were revolutionized and forever changed by the arrival of the Television.

Before its intrusion, we had radio and a record player to entertain us. I remember the record player used a speed of seventy-eight. Mom loved to play her Mario Lanza, Dean Martin, and Jimmy Rodgers albums. Dad played his Russ Colombo, Frank Sinatra, and Louis Armstrong music constantly.

These records were soon replaced by a better sounding LP that played at a speed of thirty-three, and a shorter disc with a large hole that played at forty-five. That change brought new music to our home, and soon we were enjoying The Kingston Trio, Platters, Crew Cuts, Harry Belafonte, and Nat King Cole. The reel- to-reel tape-recorder kept our parents busy for hours recording their old seventy-eight records.

As I mentioned, things changed radically when a monster disguised as a simple box with a screen appeared in our living room. Television took Panama by storm. Now, instead of playing and intermingling with our friends on both sides of the park, we rushed home and turned on the TV and did not move until it was time for dinner.

At the beginning we had to turn it off so we could sit together at the dinner table to continue what was a tradition in most households, family conversation. Everyone had an opportunity to talk about their day, bring forth issues and so forth. However, this wholesome exercise in family togetherness was doomed to go by way of the Dodo bird.

All of a sudden, just like a conspiracy, someone programmed a show during the dinner hour that Dad liked. Soon after, TV trays appeared in all the stores. From then on, it was dinner on a tray in front of the tube, and silence.

This monstrous but exiting apparatus not only broke the old stodgy family traditions, but brought confusion and unrest to our simple life. We became increasingly aware of things we never knew we needed, but now were paramount to our existence.

Inadvertently, out of this confusion came more freedom for us kids. Mom and dad preferred to watch TV without us around. At first, we only had one channel. It was in English. Our parents soon tired of us asking, "What did they say?" We were either sent off to our rooms or told to be quiet. Conversation as we knew it, ceased.

We all had our favorite programs; one of mine was the Jack Benny show. It had a black man who played the part of Mr. Benny's butler. His name was Rochester, and he was very funny. The invention of canned laughter was great. You didn't need to understand the words to know when to laugh. This show had an awful singer named Dennis Day. His song was the time for all of us to get up and go to the bathroom, gather a snack, or get a cold drink.

Our parent's influence began to decline. The more time we spent alone, the more independent we became. And, the more time we spent in front of the tube, the more we were influenced by it.

It was everyone's God-given right to smoke in those days, and that included women. They were able to acquire the right to do it in public sometime before I was born. Looking at things now, I'm sure the constant exposure to films helped the females grow the attitude it took to become totally emancipated.

It was the era of tobacco. All the adults in movies, television, and in real life walked around smoking cigarettes, consequently we kids did too, although certainly not in public. Today, at age fifty-seven, and knowing better, I am still battling that smoking culture. Real men, and sensuous women smoked, and western men smoked Marlboros. I live in Texas, I still enjoy them, but now they come in a white box instead of a red one. Talk about the lingering power of advertising.

Before we were able to find our way back towards our safe and conservative Latin roots, Elvis Presley crashed into our lives and hammered the last nail on the conformist coffin. Any chance the old traditions had of making a comeback died with the electricity that Elvis the "Pelvis" brought into our lives.

I remember the time when he was supposed to appear on the Ed Sullivan show. We were one of a few families in the neighborhood with a TV, so the house was packed with friends and neighbors. The groans that came out of the females when they realized Elvis was not going to show them his gyrating lower torso was deafening.

This American shot of energy continued. We learned to do the Twist, and use the Hula Hoop. At this point in our lives, it could be said that we were in love with all things American. The world was quickly evolving, and it had their stamp all over it.

We grew into teenagers and fell in love with Levis blue jeans and Butch hair cream. Ed Byrnes taught us to carry a comb in our pockets.

It was during our teens, when we were trying to emulate Elvis, Brando, Sal Mineo, and James Dean (in particular) that things began to change for the worst. For some unexplained reason, probably to do with politics, the gringos left Cristobal and moved across the Caribbean Sea to a place called Coco Solo. In a flash, we found ourselves by ourselves, and with ourselves. We complained, and asked our parents and teachers, "Why did the gringos leave?"

We were told (by those in charge of political knowledge) that we didn't need to worry. They hadn't gone very far, and their leaving was good for us because it gave us more territory. Well, we were not sure about how good their departure was, seeing that our girls were not allowed to wear anything tight, use red lipstick, or put on those eye-scorching short-shorts. The best they did in that department was baggy Bermuda shorts. We had also noticed, to our disappointment that now there was a huge shortage of blondes in our lives. That did not set well with us, being that we were all enamored with the likes of Marilyn Monroe, Jayne Mansfield, Mamie Van Doren, Diana Dorr, and Anita Ekberg.

Blonde hair and big breasts were indistinguishable, and indispensable in our minds. One came with the other, and we would accept no less. Nevertheless, we accepted the change and went on as best we could. Some of us, I being one of them, applied and was accepted into Cristobal High School, which was no longer in Cristobal, but now across the Caribbean Sea, in Coco Solo.

This situation brought no end of excitement to all of us

who were fortunate to enroll in CHS, because now we were imbedded in their culture. Plus, that close association brought the American girls back into our lives. Except now, instead of just looking at them, we could kiss them. And, since you couldn't kiss them without talking to them, every single one of us Panamanian kids attending school in the Canal Zone learned to speak English in record time.

Even though we were now separated by the Caribbean Sea, and a road distance not easily negotiated life between both cultures essentially remained okay. We continued to visit each other's realm whenever possible. Unfortunately, only a handful of Panamanian kids were able to attend Cristobal High. The majority of them were kept away from the Canal Zone and left to their own devices.

Time passed, and the poison tongues of opportunistic politicians hiding under the bandwagon of nationalism started to brew trouble in our city. For some reason, and I was never quite sure why, we either wanted or needed more territory.

Before long there were riots because the Americans would not leave, and a power struggle between politicians from both countries ensued. These negotiations culminated with the weak American President, Jimmy Carter, agreeing to leave the Canal Zone by the year two thousand. It was a bitter pill for all of us that desperately wanted them to stay. Still, they weren't gone yet, and that gave us solace.

We were fortunate to have a foreign culture living next door, like in Europe, and did not want to get rid of it. Besides, we could never understand who in their right mind wanted to send the American girls away.

I remember the time when Dad and I were watching one of the two Spanish channels that were now available on the tube, and were listening to this politician tell us why the Americans needed to leave. I was a senior at CHS at the time, and Dad and I looked at each other befuddled, as the movement to kick the Americans out was gaining momentum. Dad and I connected that day. It was the only time he and I ever agreed on a political platform. I had developed Mom's political stance; we were staunch liberals, and did not care for his conservative attitude. Our whole family was pro-American.

Dad was a fortunate man, being that his father had held the position of Governor of our province, and was a man of some wealth. Dad was educated in the United States, attending St. John's Military Academy, Holy Cross High School, and Villanova University. He was born with a silver spoon in his mouth and spent his entire life partying. He had the Panama-American newspaper delivered to the house every morning. It came in English, much to Mom's irritation. She couldn't read it.

Time continued to tick and soon the Zonians started to leave in droves. As they moved out, we moved in, taking over their territory until most of them were gone. Now Panama is struggling to get out from a major recession.

When the Americans left, so did their money. And, even though we were expecting their money to depart, we were unpleasantly surprised to find how much our economy depended on them.

After figuring out how much money we were going to make from the transit fees produced by the canal, and adding on all the extra business related deals pertaining to international commerce, we felt financially secured. However, we failed to take into consideration one huge factor: The domestics and grass cutters that were employed by the gringos. Thousands of Panamanians were involved in domestic work; getting paid in cash for their services, which included maids, cooks, chauffeurs, gardeners, day laborers, etc.

The Canal Zone looked like a tailored suit. Everything in its place, and a place for everything, and that meant keeping the ever-growing grass cut. There where hundreds of grass-cutters who were paid in cash. Once these multitudes were laid off and had no money to spend, the country was plunged into a devastating recession that still exists to this day.

As time let on many Panamanians left the republic. Having grown-up with the gringos next door, we were familiar with their culture. So, when it came time to decide which university was best for your child, most parents picked one in the United States. Much to their chagrin, most of us never came back. We married American girls and settled in their home state. This brings me to the nut of the story, my friend Mary Williams.

Mary was born and raised in the Canal Zone, and married

a Panamanian. When it came time for the Americans to leave the zone, she wouldn't. First of all, Panama was her country. You couldn't extract the zone from the republic if you tried. The only contact most Zonians had with the U.S. was during summer vacation when they traveled by ship to visit family members.

Mary's way of life, her food, and her culture was a mixture that could not be separated. The tropical climate, the mountains, dense jungles, enchanting Caribbean Sea, and the beautiful Pacific Ocean are imbedded in the Zonians soul. We were an extension of each other.

Their area of residence was neat, orderly, quiet, but void of color. Our side had more flavor, diversity, and excitement. But it was noisy, and lacked order.

I left Panama in November of 1964, following my mother who had been appointed Consul General of Panama in San Antonio, Texas. I pursued my university studies halfheartedly, married several American women, and still reside in Texas. Yet, each time I visit Panama, I always make a point to stop by Mary's house and see her.

While there, I ask the same two questions: "How are you getting along now that most of your friends have gone?" And, "Do you and Francisco have any plans to leave the republic any time soon?"

Mary always gives me an incredulous look, and then tells me, "Why should I leave my home? I like it here."

The last time I was in Panama, I took a taxi to her house in Balboa Heights. While eating dinner with her and Francisco, I chided her about the fact that she was fast becoming extinct, since there were fewer than two hundred Zonians left in the old enclaves, and those were scattered through the two provinces. Then, with a smile, I would say, "Ras Mary, you are going to be like the last mango on the limb."

One evening, after one of my many visits, we left the dinner table so the maid could clean up. Francisco poured us three delicious Carta Vieja Special Reserve rum & coke drinks. We sat outside, and Mary toasted to my health. Then she addressed my curiosity.

"Yes, you are right, Gunther, I'm fast becoming an oddity here. My circle of American friends is down to a handful. I can leave anytime now and move to Florida. Francisco and I have saved enough money. The trouble with that plan lies in the fact that Francisco and I have always been mangos, and regrettably, once you have been a mango, it's hard to make the transition into an orange. We have decided to stay in paradise for a while longer."

As I'm flying back to Texas, I began to reflect upon Mary's situation and wondered how the thousands of gringos raised in the Canal Zone feel about their new lives in the States. Then I reflect on my own life, and the answer hits me like a ton of bricks. *You can easily learn to like an orange, but the taste and texture is nothing like the mango.* Panama is an exotic and marvelous place, something that can't be said about Texas, Florida, or California, which is where most of the Zonians and Panamanians have settled. That world of ours that existed in yester-years is gone from us forever because we let go of the limb too early. But not Mary, she is desperately hanging on to it, squeezing out every last bit of enjoyment out of a tropical life forever lost to the rest of us. And yes, she knows quite well that her life there must come to an end. Yet, when it does end for Mary, it will not come as a shock. Paradise has a tendency to lose some of its luster when all your friends have gone.

When Mary's time is up, and she disembarks in Florida with her husband and furniture, she will be able to say proudly to those that will undoubtedly ask her, "Are you going to miss living in Panama?"

Her answer will surely be, "Nah, I was the last mango on the limb.

This story was originally written in anger after the Nine-Eleven attack. Arcia is not the type of guy who would go and throw a rock at a mosque, so he penned it as an outlet for revenge. Later, needing money, he removed the venom, toned it down, injected it with a dose of comedy and sold it to J D Publishing in Spring, Texas. Once the rights reverted, he converted the piece into a two-act stage play. The Woodlands Writers Guild sponsored the play. Philip Mintz directed it. Lead role (Rejali) by Alan Berkowitz. Produced in 2012 by Arcia, and Dave Spidel at The Owner Builder Network theater hall in Magnolia, Texas. Rated PG

Rejali and the Camel

Defeated in battle and pursued by a horde of infidels, Rejali, an Arabian warrior prince rode into the Dorrian desert without his water bag.

On the third day of his sojourn, Rejali came upon an oasis. Pleasantly surprised, he dismounted and tied his horse to a palm tree. Then he walked towards the water hole.

As he approached it, he noticed a one-hump camel sitting on his rump, leaning his back against another palm tree. The beast had his front and hind legs crossed. When the Arab knelt to take a drink, the camel spat in the water. This act infuriated Rejali since there was no reason for spitting in the water except to defy him.

He stood up, brought his sword out and walked towards the camel. "I assume you have had your fill of water already, and by spitting in the pool expect me to walk away, giving you the opportunity to drink from it again."

The camel, with a curious look, engaged the sheik. "Why do you assume that I want all the water for myself? Could it not be that this pool of water is poisoned, and I, by spitting in it, am keeping you from taking what could be a fatal drink?"

Rejali gritted his teeth. "You mean to tell me that you, who appears to be quite refreshed, have not taken a single drink from this pool of water?" Fingering the point of his sword, the Arab continued to approach the camel.

"That is correct," said the camel, totally oblivious to the menacing sword in the Arab's hand. "And, that I appear to be revitalized is nothing more than a wrongful observation from someone who is obviously unfamiliar with camels."

"What? How can you say such a thing? My name is Rejali. I am a prince. Abdullah, my older brother is the Sultan of Arabia. Furthermore, I happen to own many camels, and not a single one is as disrespectful as you are."

"You may own many," retorted the camel. "But you certainly have not spent quality time with any of them, have you?"

The Arab scratched his itchy beard and pondered the situation.

Rejali suspected he had to be delirious from the heat and lack of water, because he was having a conversation with a camel. The notion did not please him, but his curiosity needed to understand the reason for the beast insolence.

"What are you getting at?"

"I mean you came upon this oasis by chance, and on a horse," replied the camel, with a chuckle.

"By what name are you called?" asked Rejali, trying to control a surging anger towards this mouthy, and insulting beast.

"My formal name is Rigoberto, but my friends call me Rondee."

"Ha, ha, ha," laughed the sheik, "I have been in Arabia all my life and have never heard of a camel going by that ridiculous name. Nonetheless, if you mock me one more time, I will be forced to cut-off your hanging jewels, which must be fairly large to match your insolent attitude."

"Ah," said the camel, as he gently uncrossed his hind legs, stood, and spat on the sand. "How very typical of man to think that removing the cojones from an animal will make him obedient."

The Arab became puzzled. "Where did you get that name for balls?"

"I heard my cousins, the Llamas call them by that name once or thrice."

"How does a…oh, never mind," grumbled the sheik. "I must be mad from thirst to be talking to an animal."

Rejali approached the camel, slicing the air with his sword. "Animals do not talk, so you must be some kind of wizard, or maybe even a demon."

"I am not a wizard or a demon," protested the beast. "What I am is an ordinary camel named Rigoberto by my late master, who perished in a shipwreck off the Aburkian coast. Obviously, you haven't seen much of this world."

"That's it!" bellowed the Arab. "You are dead meat." Rejali raised his sword, and with unexpected quickness reached the back-pedaling camel. "Kiss your jewels good-bye."

"Wait a moment," pleaded the camel. "Can you not forgive my mockery for the fact that I might have saved your life?"

"What do you mean might have? Is this pool of water poisoned, or are you adding false statements to the list of your misdeeds?"

"I did not say it was poisoned, only that it might be. You can't be too sure around here."

The Arab looked around. "We are in the middle of the desert, for crying out loud. No one is dumb enough to poison the only water hole for leagues?"

The camel stared at the human with amusement, but kept quiet.

Rejali, angry, looked at the beast in the eyes. Then, to the camel's discomfort, a devilish grin appeared on his face. "Drink from it and I will spare your camel-hood, but if it is not poisoned, I will cut out your tongue for being a liar."

Rigoberto, sensing things were fast spiraling out of control, told the Arab he should get his horse to drink from the pool.

"But if the pool is poisoned, my horse will perish," said Rejali with anguish. "I love my horse. You, on the other hand...."

"If the water is poisoned, then I will die."

"Better you than my horse. Drink from it or face an even worse fate. A life without speech, and you know what else."

The camel, with a solemn tone spoke to the human. "Listen to me. If I die, you and your dubious ride will perish as well. And, if you don't mind me saying it, your silly horse cannot survive more than a couple of days without water, and for that matter, neither can you. In addition, since you had a look of surprise painted all over your face when you arrived, it is safe to say you were utterly lost. It can then be assumed that if I die here, you and your dippy horse will also give up the ghost. However, if I do not die, both of us can get out of here and live to tell the story. I am not only familiar with this desert, but I am a camel, and our kind can go without water for weeks."

Rejali realized this impertinent beast was right, he had no recourse but to let his horse drink first.

"What assurances do I have that if my horse dies you will not leave me here to perish as well?"

Here's the deal, said the camel. "You leave all my body parts alone, and I will not only get you out of here, I will take you to a place called paradise."

The sheik's mind was weakening. For three days he had wandered the desert without a drop of water, and although he was fairly certain he was hallucinating, he pondered the situation and agreed to the beast request. Moussa should drink first.

The Arab walked over to his horse, stroked his long flowing

white mane, hugged his neck, and kissed him on the forehead. Then he led the horse to the water. Moussa, being thirsty, drank his fill. Rejali, seeing that the water was not poisoned, drank from it. Then he jumped in it, splashed himself, and screamed with delight.

This type of behavior further lowered the camel's poor opinion of the Arab. Rigoberto refused to drink from it until the mud had settled back to the bottom, making the pool clear again.

"Just like a sheik," he mumbled. "No sense of courtesy."

"Don't push your luck," Rejali warned. "Promise or no promise, I will not tolerate endless verbal abuse from someone who is both mouthy, and devious. And lost as I may be, I have now quenched my thirst and can go on my way and find the end of this infernal desert."

"Doubt it," said the camel.

"Doubt what?"

"Doubt that you and your impractical mount can find the edge of the desert before both of you become thirsty again."

The Arab scratched his itchy beard again. Then, with suspicion, he approached the camel. "Tell me, why is it that you can talk?"

"Animals have always been able to speak. The question should be, why is it that you can understand me?"

"Right, I'll buy that. Why is it that I can understand you?"

With a serious expression, the camel spoke to the human. "It's because you are having an out-of-body experience. If you must know, I have been waiting here for you to take you to paradise."

"What? Speak clearly so I can understand you. Are you trying to tell me I'm dead?"

"You are human, and most are brain dead," said the camel with a chuckle.

Rejali was not amused at the jest, but he was not angry. Everything seemed fuzzy to him lately. He could not remember whether he got away from the soldiers that were chasing him. He did recall the sandstorm and how he lost his horse. Yet, he remembered that Moussa came back for him.

After regaining his composure, the Arab decided he could not be dead. After all, he was a Moslem prince, and when the time came for Allah to call him home, he would send down a chariot pulled by a dozen white horses. Still, he was not taking any chances. Even though he was fairly sure he was not dead, he wanted very much to remain alive. Rejali decided it was crucial to put up with this mouthy and uppity beast, at least until he was safely out of the desert.

Rigoberto finally stuck his snout in the water and began to drink.

Rejali approached him. "Do you really know the way out of here?"

Rigoberto ignored the brusque human, and kept on drinking until he had his fill. When he finished, he looked the human in the eyes. "Mount your sorry ride and follow me. If he can keep up, I will take you to paradise."

On the second day of their journey, the horse had difficulties keeping up with the steady pace of the camel. Being exhausted, Moussa stopped.

"Just like a horse," mumbled Rigoberto. "All show and no go."

The camel, after a short rest, changed direction and led them to another oasis.

Rejali rejoiced, dismounted, tied his horse to a palm tree and crouched to have a drink. Before his lips could touch the water, the camel spat in the pool.

"Aaarg," screamed the Arab. "Do we have to go through this again?"

"Only if you want to; if you don't, get your horse and give him a drink."

Rejali pulled his sword out. He was tired, angry, and had enough abuse from this crabby beast. But, as he approached the scruffy animal, he remembered he needed to control his anger if he wanted to get out of the desert alive. Killing the camel here would do him no good. There would be time for that later. He sheathed the sword, grabbed his mount by the bridle, and brought him to the water hole. Yet this time, after several mouthfuls, the horse's stomach started to heave and contract. Moussa shook violently, dropped to the ground, and began to moan in pain.

Rejali could not bear to see his faithful horse suffer any more. He unsheathed his sword and shoved it through the animal's heart. Not wanting the camel to see tears flowing from his eyes, he turned his back to the beast.

Rigoberto, trying to console him, pulled his cord. "Can you ride a one-hump camel without a saddle?"

Rejali wiped his tears dry and turned to face the camel. "Listen to me," he said with defiant pride. "I am an Arab, I can ride a camel no matter how many humps he has. And who says I don't have a saddle?"

He removed his gear from the dead horse, and after some modification, managed to adapt it to fit the camel. Then they continued on their way for two more days before the edge of the desert appeared in the distance. As they approached it, they noticed tufts of green grass intermingled with small bushes. Soon, a green meadow covered with wild flowers came into view. The Arab, weak from thirst struggled to get off the camel. He managed to walk a few steps before he collapsed.

Rigoberto looked at the bedraggled human lying on the ground with pity. He went to look for water, and soon found a nice stream. After drinking his fill, he cupped a gulp of water in his big lower lip and brought it to the dehydrated man. He dripped the water slowly on the Arab's face, and into his mouth. He did this a number of times until Rejali regained consciousness and was able to walk to the stream himself.

When the Arab regained his strength, he realized he was hungry. Rejali found a tree, broke off a branch, whittled it to a fine point, and returned to the stream. He saw a fat trout and speared it for his dinner. Before eating, he faced east, kneeled, and said his prayers.

The camel, in his usual matter-of-fact-tone asked him if he was not supposed to pray five times a day.

Rejali looked at him. "Aren't you a Muslim?"

"No, I am a Hindu camel, but I come from the Kashmiri region of India where there are many Muslims. Apparently, I must have familiar traits from my association with them, which is why you are confused."

The Arab rolled his eyes. He was almost at the end of his rope with this beast. He stared at the camel in silence.

"I know what you are thinking," said the animal. "How does a one-hump, Moslem dromedary come from a two-hump, Hindu camel region?"

"Well, actually no, I wasn't thinking about that at all," said the Arab. "But since you mentioned it, you have aroused my curiosity. I'm all ears."

Rigoberto spat on the ground, sat on his rump, and began to tell his story: "My parents came from Arabia with their masters and settled in India. My mother, heavy with me, was separated from my father and sold to a trader from a far-off land. I was born in a mountainous place called Peru. My mother was never able to get over losing my father. She failed to adapt to our new home and died, leaving me to live amongst my cousins, the Llamas. I was particularly bright as a calf, so I was sold back to the same trader, who transported me back to the Kashmiri region of India. Then, a human who owned a troupe of minstrels and performing animals purchased me. I was taught to do tricks. Sometime later, I boarded a ship with all my comrades. We were sailing toward the great Island of Malta, where we had been booked to perform before the king. Unfortunately, we ran into a storm and wrecked off the Aburkian coast. I was the only survivor. So, although I am a dromedary, and have countless Muslim friends and relatives, my adopted home was full of two-hump camels. They taught me their traditions, and schooled me in the Hindu religion. After a while, even though I was missing a hump, I decided it was best to become a camel. That is my story."

"Right," said Rejali, smiling. "Let me remind you that Allah is merciful and forgives us our forgetfulness. Praying five times a day is not always possible."

"Why were you lost in the desert? And, if your brother is really the Sultan of Arabia, why were you there by yourself?"

Rejali looked around. "I was alone in the desert for reasons that I'd rather not disclose. Nevertheless, I will tell you this much, since you seem unusually curious for a camel. A horde of armed infidels were chasing me. I chose the desert as an escape route. Not being from here, I simply lost my way."

The Arab finished his meal, turned over and fell asleep with a smile. He was thinking that if this shabby camel was indeed a Hindu, for sure he was not dead.

Morning came early. Rejali woke up, and ate breakfast consisting of leftover fish. He faced east and said his prayers. Feeling good about things in general, he asked the camel if they were really going to paradise.

Rigoberto knelt so the Arab could get on. Then, without answering him, he sped off in a southern direction.

61

After a while they came across a swamp. The camel stopped and checked the area for snakes and alligators. Seeing none, they crossed it.

Soon they came upon a valley so beautiful Rejali gasped in astonishment. The camel stopped, kneeled and said, "Here we are!"

Rejali had barely finished making camp when a bull with scrawny legs, a hump on his back, and long horns came running up.

"It's about time you came back Rondee."

"Good to see you too, Hoopa," replied the beast.

The Arab moved closer to the camel and whispered, "I thought you told me your name was Rigoberto?"

"Hoopa can't roll the "R's," so he calls me Rondee."

Rejali smiled and scratched his itchy beard.

The bull glanced at the Arab with disgust. "I can't believe you were sent into that infernal desert to bring this riff-raff back."

"Oh no," moaned the Arab, "Another insolent animal." That was it for him, he could take no more insults. He brought out his sword and was preparing to trim the bull's horns when a large bird of prey appeared in the sky.

The Bald Eagle swooped down and landed amongst them. The camel, being aware of his manners, introduced the aggressive bird to the Arab.

"Krona, let me introduce you to my errand. This is the human I was sent to fetch. His name is Rejali, and he has earned by his past deeds the right to enter and remain with us in paradise."

The big bird stretched her neck, sniffing the Arab thoroughly. "Ugh! Not another smelly human."

The Arab spat on the ground, but kept quiet.

Krona shot him a disapproving glance. "Is this the one you were sent out to get? He does not look like much to me."

The Arab spat again.

The eagle looked at the sword in the Arab's hand with disappointment. "Were you planning to do harm to someone with that metal shaft?"

The Arab spat.

Krona gave Rejali the bad-eye. "If you ever draw that sword again in order to do harm, I will personally rip the skin off your face."

Before the Arab could think of a reply, another animal came

walking up. This one was a three-toed long legged creature with feathers. It had a long neck and a duck-like bill. She addressed the Arab. "*Guten Morgen*. My name is Sheena. I am an Osterreich."

Rejali said good day, and then whispered to the camel, "What in the world is an Osterreich?"

"A Germanic Ostrich," whispered Rigoberto.

Ah," said the Arab, scratching his itchy beard. "Yes, of course. I knew that."

Sheena approached him. "You need a bath. And, what are you doing wearing a rag on your head? Don't you know it's unsanitary? We certainly need to do something about your filthy clothes, and you have to scrape off all that facial hair. You can't be carrying a habitat for lice around here."

"Oh no," moaned the Arab. "Where am I?"

The eagle butted in, "Why, you are in paradise. Didn't Rondee tell you? All wandering souls end up here. Once you have entered our realm you will never leave it."

"Oh no," cried Rejali, dropping to his knees. He opened his arms wide, and with despair in his voice, spoke to the camel. "I am dead, aren't I?"

The beast gave the eagle a disapproving look. Then he stared at the Arab for a moment. Rigoberto looked at the sky where dark clouds were beginning to gather, and then at the despondent human still kneeling on the ground.

The camel's friends left as quickly as they came, leaving him alone with the downhearted man.

"Listen to me, Rejali, it looks like a gully washer is about to hit us. Over yonder there is a cave, the only place around that affords us shelter. If we hurry we can get there before it fills up with the dregs of humanity."

"Aaarg! You can't be serious," said Rejali, standing up. "What can I have possibly done to end up here? This has to be some kind of mistake. I am a Muslim. When I die, I surely will not end up in a place like this. The Koran is explicit as to where I am supposed to go."

The camel remained silent.

Rejali stared at Rigoberto, who in turn stared back. He approached the camel and began scratching the beast on the neck. "Ah, I know what this is all about. You are playing a prank on me, aren't you? Whose idea was this? My wife sent you, didn't she? Fatima put you up to this, didn't she? Ha! Well, it will not work, so you might as well go and tell her Rejali is too smart to get snagged by such a transparent trick."

The camel looked up at the sky, then at the Arab. "We are going to get a good soaking if we don't get moving. A monstrous storm heading our way, lightning can be dangerous, we must move on."

"Ha! If we were dead you would not be afraid of lightning. You had me going there for a spell. And to think I almost fell for it."

The camel, frustrated, spoke to the human. "I never told you I was dead, and I never said you were dead, only that you were having an out-of-body experience. For all I know you could be brain dead, and that is tantamount to the same thing, is it not? Furthermore, if we do not get out of here quickly, both of us might die, if you are not already dead. The storm is dangerous, and it's coming our way. If we hurry, we can find a spot inside the cavern, and while we are there you can look for one of the priests that dwells within, and try your hand at confession. You certainly have a lot to confess, don't you?"

Rejali crossed his arms. "All right, so I cheated on Fatima once or twice. I could not help myself. After all, I am an Arab prince. I am supposed to be amorous." He looked around and lowered his voice. "The young girls I had affairs with didn't mean much to me. I will admit to their beauty, and I will confess I could not resist their charms. But you must understand that making love to them was not easy."

Rigoberto stared at the distraught human with wonderment.

Rejali looked around again, and whispered. "You don't know what I had to go through to bed them. Fatima had spies following me all the time."

"Why are you telling me this? Do I look like a priest to you? I was not informed of your evil deeds, only told to go into the desert and pick up a wandering human."

Rejali looked at the camel. "Do you suppose it could be possible you made a mistake and brought the wrong person to paradise?"

"Doubt it."

"Doubt what?"

"Doubt that I made a mistake. I never make mistakes. You are the right one all right."

Rejali spat on the ground. "Who sent you?"

"I was ordered to fetch you by my mistress, the Queen of the Over World."

"What in the name of Allah is the Over World?"

"A place you come to when your time in this world is over," said the camel with a chuckle. "Say, you might be dead after all."

"Aaarg!" screamed the Arab. "I am not dead, you brainless dromedary, but you will be if you keep this up." He brought his sword out, smiled, and fingered the edge. "Mock me one more time, and I am going to spill your blood."

"I would not do that if I were you."

"Tell me why not? Is it because of that oversize eagle? I am not afraid. Why should I be? She is not here, and I can run this sword through you and be off before she returns."

Rigoberto looked up once more. "We'd better get going. This is truly a dangerous storm. The clouds are dark, low, and seem heavy with water."

Rejali was not paying him any attention. Instead, he was slicing the air with his sword. Despairing, Rigoberto approached him with both ears flapping, and began to explain the situation: "This is not about whether you are dead or not. You don't have to be dead to be here, although it helps. It is not even about your evil deeds, although you seem to have committed more than your share. This land we call paradise is a place you end-up when the 'Almighty Goddess of Wisdom and Life' decides to remove you from those who are not like you, and cannot benefit from your company. Here, you will find yourself amongst your own kind."

"For what purpose am I here, and for how long?"

"How would I know? I am only the messenger. However, I will bestow on you this much, since you are so anxious. Not everyone in paradise is dead, although there are some that will argue the point. How long you will be with us depends on your attitude."

Rigoberto looked at the bewildered man with disgust because he had a blank look on his face. Irritated, he continued with the story: "Rejali, because of your way of life, this is a better place for you. If you can find fulfillment here, you will be allowed to leave. On the other hand, if you can't, you will be with us forever."

"You mean to tell me if I really like it here, I'm free to go anytime? But if I hate it, I have to remain?"

"Yes, more or less. I mean you can leave only when you have reached an understanding about your purpose in life, and are content with it. But when you leave paradise, if you ever do, it won't be toward the life you led…that passage is closed permanently to you."

"What exactly do you mean?" said the downhearted human.

"If you find paradise to be the perfect place for you, then you can, if you prefer, leave it. Yet, you will remain here forever if you decide this place is not at all suited for you. To further clarify your position, if for some reason you hate it here and are allowed to leave, it will not be to the place you came from. Once here, you will never find your way back home. Not really."

"Aaarg! You speak in tongues. Why must we deal in riddles? Can you not give me a straight answer?"

"What exactly is it that you want to know?"

Rejali gritted his teeth. Then he began to tremble with rage. Composing himself, he tried once more to communicate with this most annoying of beasts. "To begin with, I want to know if I'm dead. Then, I want to know in case I'm not dead, can I actually walk away from here and find my family and go home? Finally, if it's not too much trouble, I want to know why it is that here, in paradise, animals seem to be in charge of man's world."

The wind began to swirl, and lightning illuminated the sky. Keeping an eye on the weather, Rigoberto sat on his rump and wearily spoke to this irreconcilable soul.

"You are no longer alive in the sense of what life once meant to you. You will be forever here, unless by your actions that ticket is revoked. If so, you will be sent to the underworld where darkness prevails. If you refuse to become enlightened, you will find darkness sooner than you think."

Rejali had a blank look on his face.

Rigoberto spat on the ground, and leered at the ignorant Arab. "Now, as to the reason we are in charge here. We were put in man's world to provide him with the things he needed to cope, companionship and comfort being two of them. In spite of our efforts, man abused us; some of us to the point of extinction. Not all humans are cruel, and as such it is the same with animals. We are not all predators. I went through a great deal of trouble to bring you here because you were deserving of a second chance. Your deeds were not bad enough to send you straight into the abyss of darkness. And, even though the kind of life you are expected to live here is vastly different from what you are accustomed, it is much better than eternal darkness. We animals are here to help you cope with your surroundings. It's our penance. We blame our never-ending burden on the snake, but that is another story. I step on them whenever I see one, don't you?"

"What? What does a snake have to do with anything?"

The camel stood and placed his face against Rejali's. "If you persist in ignoring danger, lightning will strike you, especially if you keep that metal shaft out in the open. If that happens, your ticket to life-everlasting will be revoked, and you will get a free ride into the abyss."

Rigoberto stopped talking, turned, and without saying good-bye, broke into a full run, heading towards the cave.

"Wait a minute!" yelled Rejali, as lightning struck nearby. "What's all this talk about a ticket-to-ride? What ticket? What kind of a stupid upside down world are we in?"

The camel didn't respond, he continued to run.

Rejali fingered his sword while rain poured on him. He thought what he needed to do to get some respect in this place was to shove a bit of steel into warm flesh.

Rigoberto stopped running and looked back at the sword waving Arab. "What a pity," he mumbled. "All that trouble for nothing."

He spat on the ground and did not stop running until he reached the cave.

"Where is your errand, said Hoopa, the long-horn bull. "Why is he not here?"

"He is out there in the midst of the rain and lightning waving his sword."

The bull snorted. "Didn't you tell him lightning is a conduit to the dark side?"

"Yes I did, but he's a fanatic. He came here with a ticket-to-ride."

Written in conjunction with Ray Fitzgerald and Bob Dailey, fellow members of The Woodlands Writers Guild. It was done in a day, through e-mail, while at work. Each one penned a few paragraphs, and then sent it to the other. Rated M

The Saga of Raymond the Poor

The Award

There were church mice in the village that had more money than Raymond the Poor. In the entire kingdom of Zaroch no one was lower on the economic food chain than Raymond the Poor. If rags were riches, he would have been a financial baron. Maybe it was pity; maybe it was just helping their fellow man, but for whatever reason Raymond's fellow peasants nominated him for "Serf of the Year."

The nomination went unchallenged, and Raymond was in line for a handsome reward from Herbert the Horrendous, the Grand Duke of a fiefdom that was declared four levels below the established poverty line.

Raymond was anxiously dressing for the long trek to the Duke's palace, but he could not decide on what to wear; the ratty tattered brown pants or the faded smelly blue shirt. Choice of shoes posed no problem as he only had the one that fitted his right foot, and that one had a hole in the middle of the sole. For a brief moment, he considered asking his brother for a short-term loan to acquire some decent attire, but he quickly discarded that notion. He dreaded talking to his brother more than he feared the bubonic plague. Maybe he should try and touch his sister; she had married a blind, wealthy shoe cobbler and had ample funds to spare.

After thinking things out, Raymond decided he could not appear before Herbert the Horrendous in anything other than his usual shabby attire, after all, a man must be proud of whatever honor falls his way. Still, poverty aside, a man needs to observe the rules of propriety, and showing up with one shoe would bring him shame and diminish the affections of Ursula the Unwashed, a woman he loved dearly.

With a fast gate, he called on the blind cobbler. To his chagrin, when he made it into the shoe store, he found that all the shoes were matched, and the blind-relation would not allow him to break a pair. Upset over this development he went to see Pablo the Prophet, who also worked as a barber. The Soothsayer told him he needed to leave the village and venture forth to the land of the Right-Wingers. "Everyone there wears right shoes. Surely you could get one to match the one you have."

Disgusted, Raymond spat on the ground. "But I'm in need of a left shoe," he complained. "What good will it do me to go there? They only have right ones?"

"By golly, you're right," said the wise old codger. He scratched his ample ass, sat on a stool, and began to think. Then, an idea shot through Pablo like a bolt of lightning. "Eureka!" he said. "You can try your fortune in the land of the "Left-Wingers," surely they will sell you a left shoe. But you must be careful, it's been rumored that Robere the Rogue was seen about."

Raymond the Poor was elated at this most relevant of revelations, and thanked the Sage for his infinite wisdom. However, before he could depart, the man demanded payment.

"But I can't afford to pay you," said the poor man, with anguish. "All I have left in the world is my lucky rabbit's foot. I need it. The journey ahead appears to be quite dangerous."

His fervent pleas fell on deaf-ears; the Soothsayer demanded payment for the consultation. Reluctantly, Raymond handed over the lucky talisman. Distraught over being taken by the brazen prophet, he called on Ursula the Unwashed, said farewell, and commenced his surreptitious journey.

The Highwayman

Raymond had not ventured very far when he realized he had been duped. Money would be needed to purchase a left shoe, and he had none. Despondent, he sat on a log and began to wail.

This noise caught the attention of Robere the Rogue, a man with a dubious reputation due to a keen eye for opportunities. After confronting Raymond, the highwayman befriended him.

"What ails you, my good man," asked Robere.

With leery-eyes and winged words, Raymond explained his dilemma to the intimidating stranger.

Robere, a man of solutions, came up with one. "Listen to me, my good man. If you would enter the realm of Ivan the Impeller and bring me the shield of Sir Marion the Malcontent, I will loan you ten pence, enough to buy a left shoe. But in order to make sure you return with the shield, I will take your right shoe as collateral."

Raymond's heart sank. Ivan the Impeller lived in the depths of Gordo, a land full of avaricious merchants who would surely cheat him out of his money. If that wasn't bad enough, Sir Marion the Malcontent was a knight known for his bad disposition. Upset over the difficulty of the quest, he approached the generous but malicious bandit.

"What you ask of me is very dangerous. I would have to traverse a maze full of pitfalls. You must endow me with a word of wisdom so my spirits can uplift my courage and allow me to proceed."

"You are called Raymond the Poor, not Raymond the Imbecile," said Robere the Rogue, quite proud of his wisdom. "Now, go and fetch me the shield."

Realizing that Raymond's countenance lacked optimism, Robere decided that more prodding was needed. He looked into the poor man's eyes, placed a hand on his shoulder, and tried to lighten the poor man's load.

"Consider your plight, my good man. You have successfully navigated your way to me without being robbed of your right shoe. You have proven yourself resourceful and brave. You started with nothing and have already acquired ten pence. Besides, not all merchants in Gordo are cheats. There is an honest one. His name is Alberto the Altruistic. And this very day he is in the kingdom of Zaroch trading his goods. Now go and secure your left shoe."

Raymond the Poor said farewell to his questionable benefactor, and continued on his journey. How to traverse the country of Gordo without being robbed of his ten pence became a matter of principle. An idea struck him; he stopped his forward process, turned around and returned to his village. He went home and carefully removed an old carved box his mother, Agrippa the Aggravating had given him as a child. The box was beautifully carved, but of no real value. Inside he placed nine of the pennies; then sealed the box with wax. The tenth penny he put in his pocket. Hurrying to the marketplace, he found Alberto the Altruistic trading his wares. Apprehensively he approached the merchant, and with alacrity he begged for an audience.

"Oh, Alberto, I have but a tiny favor to ask of you."

The benevolent merchant, taking pity on the bedraggled serf granted him an audience. "Speak now, and be done quickly, for I am a man of business and not inclined to listen to idle chatter."

"Oh, Alberto. I am but a poor man, and you are a wealthy one, yet you travel to and from the land of Gordo without fear of being robbed. I can't say the same."

"Why is that my problem?" replied Alberto the Altruistic.

"It's a benefit," mumble the poor man. "I have a gift I would like to have delivered, but I am afraid of the avaricious people in your country. I am willing to pay one pence for this service."

Alberto scratched his cheek and mulled over the proposition. Then he smiled at the poor peasant. "This may indeed be the smallest return I have ever received for my services or goods. However, I am in a charitable mood today, so I will grant your request. Who's to be the recipient?"

Raymond gave some serious thought to Alberto's question. *Who should I give the gift to?* "Only two choices" he answered. Talking to himself was a skill Raymond had sharpen to perfection. He knew he owed a debt of gratitude to his fourth ex-wife, Gertrude the Grunter. After all, she had sent him the perfect birthday gift on his fortieth birthday. It was a wonderfully hand-made ash tray carved with a craftsman's precision. Perhaps she had forgotten he didn't smoke. She didn't have a terrific memory, and often got lost on her morning trek to the outdoor privy.

Recalling with disdain the repulsive sounds Gertrude used to make during their annual love making session, he mentally erased her from his gift list.

Maybe I should try giving it to my second cousin, William the Wretched; he might be the perfect recipient of the gift. "Then again," he said, continuing the conversation with him-self, "William was named "Serf of the Year" three years ago, and I never visited his hovel to congratulate him or admire the gifts that came with such a prestigious award. One of which was supposed to be a new, deluxe model, two-hole privy."

After pondering the problem, Raymond the Poor decided that the gift should be given to his good friend, Reuben the Rower. The man owned a boat that ferried customers across the 'Ooh-la-la River' and only charged two pence each way.
Reuben was known for his fairness. He never charged three pence, always two. Raymond felt that Alberto could be trusted to deliver the box. He was wealthy, and would have to book passage himself anyway.

Alberto accepted the box, promised to deliver it and said farewell.

Raymond was elated. This way he could not be robbed, at least not on this side of the river. Reuben the Rower would take him across, and would give him the box containing the seven pence, which he would need to purchase the left shoe. Feeling good about his decision, he set forth again on this perilous journey.

The Journey

Raymond had not traveled far when his bare feet began to hurt. He sat down and cursed his luck. Then, feeling sorry for himself, he began to wail again. With every tear that fell to the ground, Raymond tried to comprehend the reason for the bad things that had befallen him, starting from the point when he won the renowned "Serf of the Year" award. That honor cost him his lucky talisman, and brought Robere the Rogue into his life.

All he had wanted was a left shoe to go with his right one so he could go and visit Herbert the Horrendous, Grand Duke of the Fiefdom of Zaroch. That seemingly easy task became monumental. Now he was traveling to Gordo barefooted, and owed Robere the Rogue money to boot. If that wasn't bad enough, he had agreed to bring back the shield of Marion the Malcontent, a murderous knight. Despondent, Raymond continued to wail.

In the middle of his loud sobs, a young boy appeared by his side.

"Who are you?" said Raymond, quite startled. "Why do you go round sneaking up on people? Don't you know it's not polite? I have a mind to put the switch to you."

"I did not sneak up on you, old man," said the rude boy. "I just appeared; there is a big difference in the two."

"No one just appears," grumbled Raymond. "Unless they are some sort of demon or wizard."

"I did just appear," retorted the boy. "I am the son of Marcus the Mystic, and I was sent here by my father to assist you."

"Halleluiah," said Raymond, elated at the disclosure. "I can sure use the help of a wizard."

"And we're glad to help you," said the young boy.

"We?" said Raymond, raising an eyebrow. "Are you telling me you have a mouse in your pocket?"

"Why yes, I do. I do have a mouse in my pocket," said the son of Marcus the Mystic. "Would you like to see it?"

Raymond nodded, and the mystical boy pulled a mouse out of his pocket and carefully placed it on the ground.

"By what name are you called?" asked Raymond.

"My name is Morgus the Miniscule," said the boy, "And this

is a rare gift I'm about to bestow upon you."

The boy waved his hand three times and the little mouse turned into a really big one. In fact the mouse became as big as a horse.

"Mount this mouse. He will carry you the distance between here and the 'Ooh-la-la River.' However, you need to heed a word of warning," said Morgus. "This mouse likes to eat the fruit of the cheese plant, which grows in this area. Do not let him eat. The mouse is lactose intolerant and will develop serious stomach problems. The large amounts of methane gas produced won't harm him, but it could kill you."

With that brief bit of wisdom, Morgus the Miniscule waved his hand and disappeared. Raymond stared at the gigantic mouse. The huge mouse stared back.

"What are you looking at," said Raymond, annoyed.

"What are you looking at, you miserable peasant," replied the mouse.

Raymond gasped, and took several steps backward. "Mice don't talk," he said. "Besides, who are you to call me a miserable peasant?"

"I am called Raoul the Irreverent Rodent, and I do talk. I can also play the harmonica and know how to count to ten, but enough of this chitchat. We must be off."

"Do you really know the way to the 'Ooh-la-la River?" asked Raymond, as he climbed on Raoul's the Irreverent Rodent's back.

"No, dummy. I thought you did."

"You are certainly an impertinent rat," said Raymond.

"I am a mouse, not a rat, and I am not impertinent. I'm Irreverent. There's a big difference."

"Take the path heading east," said Raymond. "That is as good a direction as any."

They traveled for hours. There seemed to be a cheese plant at every turn of the path, and Raymond had the utmost difficulty keeping Raoul away from them.

Time passed. Being tired, and the mouse's back being soft, Raymond dozed off. When he awoke, he was horrified to find the rodent grazing on cheese fruit. With difficulty, he coaxed the large animal back onto the path.

Finally, they came to the river. On the other side Raymond

spied a boat. "That's Reuben the Rower," he said to Raoul. "We must garner his attention."

They shouted and waved their arms, but Reuben could not hear them. Dejected, they stopped yelling and sat down. At that very moment, the rodent's eyes crossed. Strange sounds came from his mouth, and a horrendous roar shook the air. In as quick as it takes to say whatever it is that takes a long time to say, a horrible smell hit Raymond's nostrils. He became lightheaded and his eyes began to water. The last thing he saw before he passed out was the ground coming at him, quickly.

The Physician

Raymond found his way back to consciousness. It felt like a volcano of pain had erupted inside his head. The pungent smell of horse manure strangled his nostrils and flooded his eyes with milk colored moisture.

"Where am I? He whimpered.

A voice from above responded. "You, my lad, are at the humble dwelling of Phineas. I'm a part-time Physician, and full time village Blacksmith.

"Phineas, will I live to be a day older?"

"Please call me "Smithy," and yes, you may live, with my help, of course," said Phineas the Physician. "And your name sir?"

"I'm called Raymond the Poor. What's wrong with me? Is it something you can cure?"

Phineas continued with his assessment of Raymond's health. He looked at the bottom of both his feet, checked his elbows, and felt his temperature. "Well, my lad. I see you are suffering from a multitude of maladies. Now, where do I start? Let's see, you suffer from constipation, aggravation, nausea, and gout. Oh, yes, you also have an infected left foot, and a not too healthy right one. And, if you don't mind me saying it, you are desperately in need of some serious dental hygiene. And it wouldn't do any harm if you would take a bath more than twice a year."

"My body odor is the result of an unfortunate recent mishap," said Raymond, offended at the suggestion. "It was just two weeks ago yesterday that I took a bath."

"That's a lame excuse, sir. You are a very ill man, and you smell incredibly bad. I can be of help, but, only if…."

"Only if what?" asked Raymond with alarm. "Can you make me well?"

Phineas removed a small piece of wrinkled parchment from inside his cape and shook it at Raymond. "This is a list of all the ingredients in my special cure-all potion that I have successfully used to heal a variety of forest creatures. I would like to try it on you, except for…."

"Except for what," queried Raymond, "You must tell me, please?"

"I'm missing a key ingredient. I have the skin of a snake, the shell of a roach, a pinch of minced toad crap, and a cup of pure swine urine. But I'm missing a slice of a dragon's tongue. Without it, my wonder cure is useless. If you can go off and somehow acquire that last item, I could cure all your ills in an instant"

"Please, Mr. Phin, I mean Smithy. I will do anything. I must reach my proposed destination in good health. I've won the "Serf of the Year" award, but as crippled as I am, and without any prior experience dealing with dragons, how can I get close enough to one without being eaten by the creature?"

"Well, my lad," said Phineas. "Here is what you must do. Take this bag, and every time you feel faint take one bean out and eat it, it will give you strength. However, these feelings are only an illusion. You will feel strong, but in actuality will remain weak and injured."

"And that's supposed to help me?"

"Yes, I do believe it will."

"How much do I have to pay you to fix me up after I get back with a piece of a dragon's tongue?" Asked Raymond, with suspicion painted all over his face.

"How much money do you have?"

"I have none," said Raymond.

"That is a false statement," replied Phineas. "You came here with seven pence in your shirt pocket. I can't believe you are trying to cheat me. It takes an odious person to lie to their physician."

Raymond placed his fingers on the outside of his pocket and felt the coins, but when he took them out there were only five. He looked at Phineas, and frowned. "I thought you said I had seven pence in my pocket."

"I did say that. You are most correct in your statement."

"Then why do I only have five pence left, what happened to the other two?" he said, while raising an eyebrow.

"I collect my fee in advance, sir. It's easier for my patients to pay me if I take their money first."

"I see," replied Raymond, spitting on the ground. "And how did you say I arrived here?"

"I didn't say. But if you ask me, I will tell you," retorted Phineas.

"I already asked you, replied Raymond, raising the other

eyebrow."

"No you did not. You implied that maybe I had told you, but in reality I had not even mentioned it. Do you want to know?"

"Yes," replied Raymond. "I would like to know if I arrived alone or with a companion."

"Where you traveling with someone?" asked the Physician.

"Yes, I was," said Raymond, tapping his barefoot on the ground.

"Well?" said the Physician.

"Well what?" asked Raymond.

"If you tell me who you were traveling with, I will tell you if he came with you."

"I was traveling with a large mouse."

"I don't know anything about that," said the physician, "but what I do know is that Frieda, the Flogger brought you. You were passed out in back of her new oxen cart."

"You don't say."

"I do say. And I will say more, if you find it to your liking," replied Phineas.

"Please, Mr. Smithy," begged Raymond. "Tell me who Frieda is. I need to know where she went, and whom does she flog? That will do for a start. Then, if you feel the need to show me some love, I would like to know why the large mouse was not with me."

"Frieda is the twin daughter of Herbert the Horrendous. She went to see a-man-about-a-horse, but will soon return. She seemed quite taken with you. Frieda has the enviable job of flogging those who have fallen from grace. Have you fallen from grace?" asked the medicine man.

"I should think not," replied Raymond, somewhat annoyed at the suggestion. "Do you see any flogging marks on my back?"

"Humm," mumbled Phineas. "You are right, once again. Now, let's talk about this large mouse. You were with no such company. Are you mental?"

"Well, I guess! I have accepted the chore of acquiring a piece of a dragon's tongue. You could say that I'm an unbridled lunatic."

The Kiss

"Ah, there you are," said the ugliest woman in the world. "My sweet Banshee has awakened from his slumber. Kome to Frieda and give her a big juicy kiss," said a gargantuan hairy babe.

She sat upon a stool and opened her arms, beckoning Raymond. "Kome to Frieda and give her a big wet sloppy kiss," she repeated.

What could Raymond do? What began as a simple quest to acquire a left shoe had now become a task beyond his natural power.

Yet Raymond was no slacker, he was a man on a mission. Buckling up his courage he decided that valor might outweigh discretion, and prepared to embrace Frieda the Flogger. *After all, how bad could it be?* He held his breath, closed his eyes and tried to think lascivious thoughts to rouse himself to the task. He stiffened as Frieda folded her arms around him and dragged his head toward her heaving breasts. He kept his eyes tightly shut, and continued to hold his breath.

When Frieda's hands moved lower down his torso, cupping her hammy-hands around his codpiece, he panicked. Not being able to hold his breath any longer he exhaled and prepared to smell her nauseous scent. Yet, instead of smelling something like pig's sty, he smelled the scent of roses.

Apprehensive, Raymond opened his eyes. Instead of hairy arms caressing him, now lovely white limbs held his manhood. His eyes slowly took in the slim arms and followed them up to a slender and exquisite neck. Lovely, golden curls caressed the neck. As his eyes moved up again, he saw the most angelic face he had ever seen. The woman's lips were red and slightly parted. A finely formed nose above that, and then two wondrous blue eyes; the kind of blue he had seen only in the morning sky. He looked down and the filthy rags she had been wearing were now a diaphanous-gown, and he could see her nipples clamoring for him through the thin fabric.

Raymond gazed at Frieda's face. She was smiling; amused at the rise her delicate hands were getting from his codpiece.

"Frieda, you are absolutely beautiful," he said, gushing. "How did you do it?"

"My name is not Frieda the Flogger, I'm Stefana the

Stunning, and yes, I am beautiful aren't I? I have nothing but mirrors in my castle; I like to admire myself. Do you think I'm vain?"

"Not at all," said Raymond, elated at the growing groin sensation. "You're a pillar of humbleness. Did you say you live in a castle?"

"Yes I did. Why do you ask?"

"Because I never kissed a girl that lived in a castle before, do you think it will bring me good fortune?"

"Why, yes, it will. Kissing me will undoubtedly bring you good fortune. And, as far as how I did it. I went to M.I.T."

"M.I.T.?" Said Raymond, befuddled.

"Yes, the Machiavellian Institute of Transformation. I learned how to transform myself into other personalities. But there is a glitch, I can change from Stefana to Frieda right way, but transforming back from Frieda to Stefana is not as easy. Someone has to kiss me. For several days I have been a hag until your kiss brought me back to my beautiful self again, but enough history, we march to the point. My father has sent me looking for you. You are scheduled to receive the "Serf of the Year" award in a fortnight. Now that I have found you, you need to ride with me to the castle. I have a six oxen harnessed cart. I really wanted the deluxe model, but father said it was too expensive."

"You don't say."

"Yes, and I will say much more; like drag your miserable, odor reeking body onto the rear of the cart so we can leave for Zaroch."

"But I am ill," wailed the wretched man. "Phineas has told me I have an incurable decease that can only be cured if I bring him a piece of a dragon's tongue."

"That's silly talk," she said. "Whatever is wrong with you can't be cured by being eaten alive. You will live longer if you ignore the ignoramus. He sends you to your death. You better come with me."

"But I need to fulfill a quest," cried Raymond. "I have to steal the shield from that malicious knight, that pillar of loathing, Marion the Malcontent. I have to give it to Robere the Rogue, he loaned me ten pence and kept my right shoe. I came here looking for a left one."

"How comical you are," said Stefana the Stunning, giggling. "Robere the Rogue's job is to rob people; he's not a money lender."

"He did lend me money, and he took my shoe for collateral."

"You are such a funny man. I know father will love your company. He likes a storyteller, and yours are whoppers!"

"So, you think my stories are illusions? Did I tell you I was in the company of a rude mystic child, and a rather large mouse before you came into my life?"

"Please, cease and decease with all this nonsense, we have a long way to travel. And, if you persist in making me laugh, I will become enamored with you and then we will have to fornicate."

"Did you say laughing makes you want to do it?"

"Yes, I did. So please stop making me laugh. If we mate, then we will be together for the rest of our lives. Don't you have a woman waiting for you at home?"

"Humm, yes I do," said Raymond, tapping his barefoot on the floor of the oxen cart. *What do I do about this dilemma?* He remembered swearing to his beloved, before he left that he would return with a proper left shoe, and then she could accompany him to the "Serf of the Year" award's ball." Yet here he was, gone from home for only a short time and already willing to break his promises by the hand of this beautiful voluptuous woman, who would copulate at will if he just told her another funny story. *What to do, what to do?*

Raymond was many things; but a cad he wasn't therefore he resigned himself to being a serious fellow. He asked Stefana if she knew where he could find Sir Marion the Malcontent, he needed to obtain the shield.

"Not really," she said. "That is also a losing proposition. "The man is a terrible chap; he kills everyone he comes across. Why not just buy a shield?"

"Humm," mumble Raymond. "Do you suppose Robere would know it wasn't the real one?"

"I'd be willing to bet no one alive can make that distinction," said Stefana.

"But how about my left shoe?" he moaned. "I need it to go along with my right one."

"Listen to me, Raymond, you're barefooted. You need both, a right and a left one. Now, if I'm not mistaken, my brother Rupert the Ranger keeps a pair of hunting boots in the covered box of my wagon. If they fit your feet, they are yours to keep. And, as far as where to get a shield, I know of a place that sells used things, and it always has an ample supply of shields, as well as helmets, swords, and lances for sale."

Elated beyond belief, Raymond opened the box top and found the prize. Yes sir, right there under the saddle blanket was a nice pair of brown ankle high leather Ranger hunting boots. He tried them on and they fit him perfectly. Raymond climbed on board the back end of the oxen cart, and soon they were off for Zaroch.

The Trade

Halfway to the fiefdom of Zaroch, and before they made it to the 'Second-Hand' store, the travelers were accosted by Robere the Rogue who immediately demanded their valuables. Recognizing Raymond, he asked for his due.

"I was unable to obtain the shield from Marion the Malcontent," said Raymond, in a most apologetic tone, "but I have something more valuable to trade you."

"What does a poor man like you have that would interest me?" said Robere, while his wandering eyes feasted on the hot babe driving the oxen cart.

"If you would let me out of the debt, I can tell you how you can have your way with this beautiful woman without having to fight her. She is the twin of Frieda the Flogger," said Raymond in a whisper. "I hold the secret to her caresses."

"You do?"

"Yes, that's what I just said. I hold the secret, and once you have it, she's yours forever." And, if I can have the oxen and cart, I will throw in Frieda the Flogger into the deal. She can be useful if you ever want to flog someone."

"An even-Steven deal?" said Robere, intrigued at the proposition. The buxom babe manning the reigns had lots of sex appeal. "Tell me more about it."

"Come closer, and pay attention to my words," said Raymond. "Tell Stefana the Stunning the story of the Irishman, the Frog, and the Pot O' Gold. And please don't blow the punch-line. When the story is done, find a soft patch of grass because you will have a sexually ravenous woman in your hands."

Raymond and Robere looked at Stefana; she was becoming inpatient and began to fiddle with her skirt and curls.

"How exactly does this two-for-one-woman-deal works?" The highwayman wanted to know.

"Listen to me," said Raymond, "If you agree to it, I'll give you instructions. You need to trust me on this."

The bandit scratched his cheek and thought about the proposition, thinking it was a good one, he accepted it.

Raymond Returns

It was dusk when Raymond rode into his village. Everyone came to look at him. He did not seem to be the same man that had left. This Raymond was sitting proud in a wagon driving a team of six oxen. To their astonishment, he was wearing a nice pair of brown leather Ranger hunting boots, and attached to his belt was a money pouch holding several coins. His love, Ursula the Unwashed came out of her hut and fainted when he saw her man looking so spiffy. However, she soon regained her composure, and love action quickly ensued.

The following evening they were received at the castle of Herbert the Horrendous, where Raymond was honored as "Serf of the Year." He was happy to receive the honor, gave a glorious acceptance speech, and otherwise behaved un-serf like.

. After the party, Herbert accosted him. "What happened to you out there? You have changed? And where did you get the Ranger hunting boots, they're hard to come by?"

"Well, Herby," said Raymond. "It just shows you that you can take a peasant out of his village, but you can't take the village out of him. And because of that, I earned the Ranger boots."

"You don't say?" said Herbert.

"I do say," replied Raymond. "Being true to myself is how I got to where I am today."

Herbert the Horrendous was not particularly bright, but he knew a wise saying when he heard one, and Raymond had just told him the secret of his success. The Grand Duke gained an additional measure of admiration, and henceforth gave Raymond a stipend of twenty pence a year.

This newfound wealth elevated his status in the fiefdom, he was no longer known as Raymond the Poor. From here on, he was called Raymond the Rich and Righteous. And, from that day on, on any given Sunday, from the podiums of the holiest of churches across the land, priests would spread the word to burgeoning minds.

The holy-men preached, stomped, and pointed to their humble flocks that Greed, Lust, and Debauchery were pitfalls created to ruin the bravest of men. They pointed out that Raymond, a simple man had left his village to wander a sinful world, but because he was a simple man, he returned unspoiled and rich.

"Yes," they shouted from the vantage of their pulpits, "Raymond was a man with a destiny."

Raymond accepted his accolades well. He married Ursula, became an Elder, and remained in the village.

In spite of bringing forth six children into the world, he and Ursula lived happily ever after. And this last statement is no lie!

If a man is from Mars and a woman comes from Venus, how can they communicate? Written during a period of marital melancholy - After an attempt to please a woman Arcia loved...misfired.
Rated PG

The Player Piano

Once upon a time there were three wise men and a beautiful, whimsical woman. This is their story.

The first wise man was named Lupo. He was blessed with a good heart and an uncomplicated mind. The second was Michel. He possessed acumen for business, therefore had deep pockets. The third one was Ian, a man with particular skills, plus a keen eye for opportunities. The capricious woman's name was Hanna, and she had a rousing physical form.

The three men came from Europe, although separately. Each one, in his own manner arrived in the United States pursuing the coveted American Dream. Hanna lived in the city of Beaumont, in the great state of Texas.

Lupo came from the southern part of Italy and settled in a small town in Texas called Magnolia. Michel came from France, and he settled with his wife and children in a town named Lafayette, in the state of Louisiana. Ian was an Englishman residing in Stone Mountain, Georgia.

In the 1970's, during the long and difficult recession that gripped the United States, two of them had a chance encounter. Fate brought Lupo and Hanna together. He met her while attending a party at the house of a friend. Hanna was a divorced woman with two young daughters. In spite of the obvious fact that she had no interest in him, he, taken by her beauty and gaiety, swore she was the girl for him.

Immediately after the encounter, he began to work on a plan. He decided to invest money and attention on the young girls. The idea of courting Hanna through her daughters appealed to him.

He sent the girls flowers and candy to their home and school once a week, creating a favorable impression on the kids and their mother. After several months of wooing the children, Lupo was finally able to approach Hanna directly. He asked for her hand in marriage, but she was disinterested.

It was after, and certainly not before he showed some prowess in the kitchen by making an ingenuous and delicious chicken soup, that she accepted his proposal. Soon after they were married.

Hanna was happy at first. The change of venue from the city to the country suited her, and the girls very well. They loved their new home, new life, and new friends.

However, time alters everything, and Hanna's smiley face soon changed. When he inquired as to why her happiness had taken a step backwards, he was told, to his mortification, that she didn't like winter. It turned out that Hanna's had a questionable fortitude. Her cheerfulness resembled the weather.

December rolled in. The sparkle in her eyes dimmed, her gaiety collapsed, and a cold demeanor engulfed her.

Lupo was beside himself. It would take three months for winter to give way to spring. Not knowing what to do about his wife's disposition, he asked her if there was anything he could do, or get her that would help cure the sad-eye-sickness afflicting her.

Hanna smiled, her eyes sparkled, and her cheeks showed color. Yet, this reaction was short-lived. However, while under its glowing influence, she spoke to him with winged words.

"I love music. When I first married, my husband owned musical instruments. But after the divorce, the girls and I have been so poor we have never been able to afford a piano, or music lessons for that matter. The luxury of owning a player piano has been for us but a dream. If I owned one, its music would surely gladden my heart."

Lupo's jaw dropped, the reality of her words crushed him. He was not a man of means, but a hard worker eking out a decent living in the produce business. A player piano was an instrument that required serious money. Nevertheless, Lupo was a wise man -- his wisdom being a byproduct of his good heart. His emotions conveyed the notion that if Hanna could be pleased, she would love him always.

Lupo was also blessed with a tenaciousness that allowed him to achieve most goals. Armed with these qualities, he prepared to tackle the countless disappointments and obstacles that would surely try to keep him from acquiring his wife's unusual desire.

He ignored those who told him this quest was beyond his meager means. He worked diligently every day taking care of his business and spent every available free moment going through the local newspapers, trying to locate this most precious of musical instruments. Much to his regret, there were none-to-be-found that were not new, and a new one was out of the question.

In spite of this set back, he did not relent in his pursuit. Instead, he expanded his search to include publications and contacts outside his region.

Meanwhile, his beloved Hanna continued to be afflicted by an irritable sad-eye-sadness. She hardly spoke to him anymore, and even though they shared a common bed, they did not enjoy any personal warmth.

Moved by a desire to satisfy his wife's wants and needs, Lupo did something drastic. He quit his job as Produce Manager at Donato's Grocery and prepared to travel and hunt for the elusive player piano.

So, it is said (by those who claim they knew) that on a cold and grim day during the month of January, Lupo, upon hearing from his good friend, Michel, set forth on a journey. He drove his old but reliable Chevy pick-up truck down Interstate Highway 10 East. When he crossed the Sabine River, he entered the state of Louisiana. He continued past Lake Charles, and kept on motoring until he reached the city of Lafayette.

Michel, being Lupo's good friend, provided him with food and shelter. He offered him the back bedroom in his family's home, a nice room with a private lavatory. He also offered him a job in the family's bakery business.

Lupo accepted the offer because money was needed. The price of that which Hanna most desired was bound to cost more than what he was able to bring.

There are many in Lafayette who will swear that Poupard's Bakery made the best bread in town, but Lupo disagreed. He knew better. After all, he was an Italian from the south, and they were bread lovers. Without a doubt, no one made French loaves better than Michel's Bakery.

Lupo was a decent, hard-working man. Men such as him have a tendency to miss their wives and homes. To achieve his goal faster, he began to take on extra work during the weekends. When he was not working in the bakery, he was harvesting crawfish in Breaux Bridge, or working in the Boudin kitchens of Opelousas.

He saved his money diligently, except for a bottle of grappa he would purchase on a regular basis at Lombard's Fine Wines & Spirits, every Friday night. And, on occasion he would take a chance and wager some of his money at the cockfights in Carencro.

He finally managed to save half the money needed, and, as was the plan, Michel loaned him the other half. Lupo was elated beyond belief. The love he had for his beautiful Hanna was overwhelming.

Filled with joy, he sang with the radio as he drove to the house where the woman selling the used player piano lived. Being the good businessman that he was, Lupo asked her to turn it on so he could hear it.

He became miffed when he saw her sit on the bench and began to play a short version of Barcarolle. The piano, as it turned out, had been converted from a player to a regular one.

Cursing under his breath, he bought the piano nonetheless. Yes, he did remember that Hanna asked for a player piano, but surely a regular one would be fine.

The woman's two sons helped him load the instrument of music into the bed of the truck. He paid the money, bid them farewell, and off he went.

In a state of apprehension, and feeling uncomfortable with the non-player piano he had just purchased, Lupo made a right turn into Johnston Street during rush hour traffic. When he abruptly swerved, trying to avoid a stressed driver who kept changing lanes, the piano fell off the truck and shattered into many pieces.

Curses! He said quite a few, as he saw that which Hanna most desired, broken and scattered all over the pavement. To his surprise, many a fellow came to him without having been asked, and helped put the broken piano back into the truck.

It took him forever to drive the last two miles of Johnston Street. The truck kept slowing down as it came closer and closer to Michel's Bakery. He was humiliated. The stupidity of not tying the piano was going to be hard to explain.

The bakery loomed ahead. Lupo's hands were getting sweaty, and his heartbeat was rapid. *Oh! What can I possibly say to him? How do I explain the appearance of this broken musical apparatus?* After stressing over it, Lupo understood there was nothing he could say, except the truth.

He swallowed his damaged pride and told Michel the whole incredulous story.

Michel put his hand on Lupo's shoulder and smiled. "It's okay," he said. "I have a place where we can store it until it can be fixed."

Michel met Lupo years ago while they worked in a winery in the north of Italy. There they had become good friends. During their scarce time off, they used to sit outside the American Cafe, in the town of Borgomanero, sipping espresso and talking while looking and admiring the pretty girls that walked about the plaza. They talked constantly about the possibility of immigrating to the United States, where it was presumed they would not have to work so hard to make a decent living.

It was Michel's success in Louisiana that prompted Lupo to follow his dream and immigrate to Texas.

Michel did not make a fuss over the incident, although he felt some pain due to the considerable sum of money he had invested in the broken piano. Still, expense aside, he sensed the depth of Lupo's emotional wound and tried to ease the agony by being gentle with the situation. There was no need to chastise his friend. Michel decided it was best to commiserate with his agony, and he did so.

A few nights later, these two friends went out for an evening walk. They stopped at Alma's Cafe and ordered a bottle of red wine. Michel was a wise man because he had a good heart and deep pockets. He also possessed a strong sense of benevolence. These qualities were of the utmost importance, since money was first needed to buy, and now to repair Hanna's piano.

It was while they were sipping their wine, and mulling over their predicament that Ian entered the picture. Having overheard them speak about their misfortune, and noticing that his wine glass was as empty as his pockets, he joined in the conversation.

Ian was a repairman, and skill was needed to fix the wrecked musical apparatus. He offered his services

The Englishman followed the Frenchman, and the Italian into a dark, damp, warehouse where the beastly piano lingered.

Upon seeing it, Ian uttered a few words of anguish and then

93

quickly contracted a sum of money.

Ian was a wise man because he had a good heart and technical skills. Plus, he had a keen eye for opportunities. The Englishman gave them a guarantee he would return the beauty that once belonged to this seemingly ugly, and scarred instrument of music. He also promised to make it play again.

So, on a rainy week in mid-March, these three wise men joined together and started to work on Hanna's broken converted player piano.

Ian had honed his skills in a piano factory in Birmingham, England. He became distraught when he lost his American wife to a drowning accident in the Trent River. He quit his job, sold his belongings, and brought her body back home to Stone Mountain for burial. In order to avoid the cost of expensive motels, he stayed with his late wife's spinster sister, a woman void of physical beauty, but in possession of an admirable personality.

As it often happens with lonely people, one thing led to another, and they proceeded to live together. Ian eventually married her and started a new life. He also started a new career. He took a position working as a traveling salesman for an English company, selling Lucas electrical automotive parts. That is how he happened to be in Lafayette.

The collaboration of heart, money, and knowledge proved to be a successful one. Soon beauty sprouted where ugliness had previously reigned. The piano, as Ian promised, once again uttered sounds of music, although not quite as sharp as before.

These three wise men, being satisfied with their efforts, shook hands, embraced, and parted company.

Lupo arrived home ten weeks to the day he had left. Hanna and the girls rejoiced at his homecoming, especially with such a magnificent piano tied securely to the bed of the truck. Lupo's friends and neighbors came over and helped him move the heavy instrument of music to a prominent place.

Hanna's joy was such that her eyes sparkled. Yet, it didn't take long for a worrisome look to come over her countenance. The lack of a visible mechanical pump, or an electrical cord loomed as an ominous sign.

A year later, on a cold and dreary Sunday afternoon in the

middle of December, Lupo, to his chagrin, noticed that the same sad-eye-sickness was afflicting his beloved wife again. She was lying on the sofa with her far-away eyes.

He passed by the piano and inadvertently dropped a quarter on the wood floor. When he bent over to pick it up, he noticed the cobwebs on the musical device. The vision struck him to the quick and took him back to the heated argument he had with Hanna the day he arrived from Louisiana, and she found out that the piano did not play, but had to be played.

He cursed, but could not fault her for his discomfort. He knew where to place the blame. He had made a big mistake, and it wasn't going to Louisiana. The odyssey of the piano did not bring joy into his troubled marriage. What it brought was a keen sense of disillusionment. Expectations being what they were, both Hanna and Lupo were left empty and bitter.

He picked-up the quarter and placed it into the small pocket of his blue jeans. He looked at his wife's listless body, swore under his breath, lit up a smoke, and left the house. As he walked away, Lupo allowed a faint smile to grace his face. The whole miserable ordeal had not been without benefit. He had learned that marital unhappiness could be tolerated if you have friends to drink red wine with, and a bar within walking distance where you can sing and throw darts after work.

Written years ago to record his fading memories. Rated PG

The Black Christ of Portobelo

Julia Watson was a storyteller of the highest quality. While in my family's employment, she touched me in many ways. I credit her for opening my sense of wonderment. Her stories of the black arts, which I later understood to be Voodoo, and her tales of the Tuli Vieja, which was an old Panamanian woman with a chicken leg, both terrified and fascinated me. This creature grabbed mischievous children and ate them.

Julia was our laundry maid, and she did her labor in the back end of the lower floor of the house. She preferred to work alone, always running us kids away from what she considered to be her domain.

She was an older woman with a no-nonsense look about her, and because of it, she commanded our respect. Being the boy that I was, I fell into the habit of hanging around her area when my parents were busy. She liked to sing calypso songs in English when she ironed, and she always talked to herself while doing the wash. Even though I didn't understand English, I loved to hear it spoken, especially with a musical tune.

Although I kept a safe distance most of the time, trying to mind her self-imposed borders, she caught me from time to time. At first she would scold me for intruding on her privacy. Later, she relented and allowed me to approach her.

One rainy day, as was the norm, my parents had retired to the bedroom. I went downstairs to converse with Julia. I enjoyed her company, listening to her incessant talk. Out of the blue, she told me she was leaving the family's employment. I did not ask her why. Being a kid with keen ears for gossip, I already knew the reason. Out of respect for her memory, I will not disclose her motives for leaving. She rewarded my tenacity by letting me get close to her, and opened my mind to many wonderful things, fantasy being one of them.

Several days before Julia went away, she kissed me on the forehead, allowed me to rub her feet with a lotion she loved to use called Bay Rum. While engaged in the task, she told me the story of the Black Christ of Portobelo.

   She left us soon after that encounter, and for years I carried some resentment towards my father, and grandmother. They were wrong in how they dealt with her, but I could not express my feelings. In the 1950's a boy did not speak against his parents in public or in private. And grandparents were revered. So, while I'm burdening you with a story in which its mystery will not be revealed, at least not bluntly, let me at least give you the satisfaction of the backstory of the Black Christ of Portobelo.

   The statue presently resides in the Church of San Felipe, in the small port town of Portobelo, which is located in the province of Colon. In the eighteen years I lived in Colon City I was never able to see it. The roads to get there were impassable during the rainy season, and in the province of Colon the rains started in April and lasted until November.

   During the dry season the road to Portobelo was riddled with pot holes, and was treacherous at best. To drive there you needed a car you didn't mind beating up and my dad loved his 1948 Dodge Coupe. The only sure way to get there was by boat, but the opportunity never came. My father was not the adventurous type, and I was forbidden to make an attempt without an adult family member. We were raised to be obedient, and that obedience was like a restrictive chain around our legs.

   In 1964, on the eve of my eighteenth birthday, after graduating from an American High School in the Canal Zone I left for the United States with my mother and sisters. I returned in 1975, and again in the dry season of 1978. It was during the latter visit that I first laid eyes on this most fascinating of statues.

   In 1975 I drove from Texas to Panama in a German made VW Bug with my second wife and her two young boys. I cannot speak highly enough about these type of cars. Ours took everything the Pan-American Highway in Mexico, and in Central America threw at it, and arrived in good shape. However, I'm sorry to say my mental state, as well as my marriage took a beating. Driving that distance with a quarrelsome wife and two unruly step-kids that refused to get along was indeed a challenge, one that I dealt with poorly.

   It took us ten days to get to my hometown. We moved in with my father. Soon after, I was able to land a job in the American

Canal Zone. We placed the boys in a local private Catholic school, and after a spell moved into a nice rented apartment in old Cristobal.

Before the rainy season began in earnest I took the family to the town of Portobelo, crossing a river that had lost its bridge during the previous monsoon. We did it by finding passage through a shallow area. Let me enlighten you about VW Bugs. They do float. Anyway, we arrived in Portobelo and saw the statue for the first time.

Let me tell you that I'm not a big statue guy. However, this one moved me. Seeing Christ portrayed with dark skin caught my curiosity and made me smile. I was expecting him to have the black slave look, but he didn't. Instead he had a dark Moorish appearance. I couldn't help but notice this statue had captured a more realistic look of Jesus. After all, he was from Palestine, in the Middle East, yet we always see him portrayed as a white European.

I spoke with some of the locals who were selling religious souvenirs outside the church. They had a slightly different twist to the story Julia had enchanted me with. I decided to combine both versions, and add my own personal touch to it.

Now, if you do not mind, I would like to set the story up with a little historical background. This information is important.

During the reign of the Spaniards, years after the conquest of Mexico by Hernando Cortez, and of Peru, by Francisco Pizarro, a period of prosperity fell upon the Spanish realm. The gold mines of Peru were turning out the precious metal by the ton. The gold was melted and molded into bullion. It was then moved by ship to Panama City, on the Pacific side, where it was stored in fortified warehouses. It remained there until it could be transported via 'El Camino Real' (Royal Road) by heavily guarded mule caravans to the port of Portobelo. There it was stored again until the Spanish Galleons arrived to transport it to Spain.

The Spaniards built four strong fortresses, and seven minor fortifications to protect the harbor and warehouses from marauding pirates and corsairs.

The first fortune seeker to successfully attack and sack Portobelo was an English pirate named William Parker. He took it in 1602 - The last one was British Admiral Edward Vernon, of Mount Vernon fame. He destroyed it in 1739 during a mini war between Spain and England dubbed, "The War over Captain Jenkins

Ear."

This war was the result, amongst other things, of a minor, alleged confrontation between the Spanish Coast Guard, and the Captain and crew of the Glasgow brig, "Rebecca."

The story recorded by the English stated that Captain Jenkins, while sailing in the Caribbean Sea was stopped and boarded by the Spaniards. The captain and crew were mistreated. And then, without provocation, the Spaniards cut off one of Captain Jenkins ears with a knife.

There were no major battles fought during this conflict. The declaration of war led to the dispatch of Anson's squadron with orders to attack the coast of South America. Admiral Vernon, who was part of Anson's squadron, was ordered to take his fleet and attack Spanish territory in the Caribbean theater.

In the year 1668 the English Corsair, Sir Henry Morgan attacked the town from what was believed to be an impenetrable jungle. Morgan surprised the Spaniards. They were not expecting an attack from land. The pirates killed the soldiers, burned the town, and stole the gold.

Another famous English Corsair, Sir Francis Drake also made his presence felt by establishing his headquarters on what is now called Drake Island, a place not too far from Portobelo. But the jungles of Panama must be taken seriously, and Drake paid a dear price for his choice of residence. He acquired a bad case of dysentery, and died.

The town of Portobelo was rebuilt each time it was plundered and destroyed. Finally, the Spanish reigning monarchs decided that enough was enough and moved the warehouses to another place. Portobelo lost its importance and soon became forgotten. Eventually, it emptied of people, becoming nothing more than a large fishing village.

Time passed, the Spaniards lost control of their colonies at the hand of the great Venezuelan liberator, General Simon Bolivar. Panama became a province of Colombia. It was during this transitional period that the Black Christ entered the picture.

The story of its arrival in Portobelo varies, depending on which side of the isthmus you reside. However, I am not going to burden you with the many sides of this tale, instead I will give you mine and Julia's version.

***

One day, two freed slaves happened to be fishing in the Caribbean Sea in their *cayuco* when one of them spotted a wooden box floating. They rowed and snagged it, towing it into town where they turned it over to the local magistrate for safe-keeping.

The day finally came when the box was to be publicly opened. A curious crowd gathered. When the content was revealed, a collective gasp arose. It was a statue of Jesus of Nazareth. That in itself did not caused the multitude to murmur, it was the look of the statue. Jesus was portrayed as a black man.

You can imagine the kind of reception a dark skinned Jesus brought to a white community. No one was amused. They didn't want it. There was an outcry about this Black Christ being a bad omen and coming to their village to preside over their death.

At this particular time, a major epidemic of cholera was spreading rapidly through the isthmus.

The two men that found it, along with all the other blacks and Indians living in the proximity felt the statue had arrived to protect them from the disease consuming the entire province of Panama. After a heated debate, the fact that a statue of Jesus Christ had appeared, albeit black, and in a box to these two black men created the notion of it being heaven sent.

The whites soon relented and joined the blacks and Indians in prayer. They promised to honor the statue by building it a church and creating a holiday if they were spared the ravages of the epidemic. The disease consumed the whole of Panama, killing thousands except in the town of Portobelo. It bypassed the community completely.

Word of the miracle soon spread. The Cartaginians, who were the original owners of the statue contacted the local authorities and took the necessary legal steps to reclaim their property.

Several attempts were made by the authorities to send it back, but every time they tried to move it, bad luck came upon those who were involved in the effort.

The first time, as the story is recorded, the statue was placed in a box. Then it was loaded into a ship. Soon things began to go wrong, requiring lengthy and costly repairs. Then the weather refused to cooperate, keeping the ship anchored in port.

The captain, who like everyone else in those days was superstitious and had heard of the statue's miracle refused to sail with it. He ordered his men to put the statue back on land. The weather cleared the following day, allowing the ship to sail.

A record of a second and third attempt exists. The local authorities decided to remove the statue by land the second time. They strapped it to a donkey, and placed it in a caravan that was about to leave for Panama City. However, not long after it left the caravan was set upon by bandits. They stole everything except the statue, which found its way back to the town still strapped to the back of the donkey.

Later on, a third attempt was made. They were going to try the sea again. During a clear and sunny day, the authorities loaded the statue on board a ship. The town's people, with tears in their eyes waved it goodbye.

Sometime after clearing the harbor a storm came out of nowhere, lashing the ship and causing the superstitious sailors to dump the boxed statue overboard. The current carried it back into Portobelo.

At this point, the people of the town, as well as the authorities came to the obvious conclusion the statue did not want to leave. They kept it, fighting off all legal attempts by the owners to get it back.

***

Let me be fair here. When I asked a member of the historical society, in Panama City what was the real deal here, he told me the wooden statue was originally white, and because the box floated on the sea for a period of time exposed to heat and humidity, it turned dark. Rubbish, I say. I saw it, and can tell you it had a definite Moorish look.

There are a number of nonbelievers that will tell you the main reason Portobelo was spared the ravages of cholera was due to its seclusion. They also say the reasons for the statue's unwillingness to leave the town of Portobelo had all to do with unpredictable weather, and a creative priest not unwilling to deal with sabotage and bribes. It had nothing to do with holy intervention. That being said, I must add that since the Black Christ arrived in Portobelo, the residents have avoided epidemics, and not a single hurricane, earthquake, or natural disaster has befallen them.

The statue is presently enshrined in the Church of San Felipe, coming out only on the religious festival week of October 21st. It is then carried upon the shoulders of the believers, as it makes the rounds of the town in a procession.

Now, try to wrap your mind around this. For all the fame and historical value this statue has for Panama, and with all that it means to the residents of Portobelo, you can actually walk into the church, since it is always open during daylight hours and get within two feet of it. It's unguarded! The townspeople's faith is so strong they believe no one can take their Black Christ away.

If you ever find yourself in this backwater area of Panama, and try to get into the church to see this most unusual statue of the Christ of Nazareth, please take notice (if you are a female) that you must be properly dressed. Shorts and halter-tops will get you thrown out by the resident priest, if he is around to catch you.

Decades have passed since Julia left my family's employment. I still remember her facial expressions, her gentle touch, and her expressive eyes. My reluctance to stand up and argue on her behalf had nothing to do with being passive and all with being a boy brought up in an era where house workers were expendable. When the decision was made to send her away, I turned my back, put the unpleasant episode behind, and buried myself in boyhood dreams.

If the Muslims get virgins when they die, the Christian faith should offer a competitive reward. The story line in "In Search of High Ground" - The Amorous Antics of Alex Perez depicts and follows the author's sense of spiritual purpose. Rated M

Pearly Gates Brothel And Rum Bar

I woke-up on a beach. I looked around and wondered how I got here. Then I remembered the shipwreck, and being tossed overboard. The current must have washed me here.

The fog began to lift, exposing a body of resplendent water. *Hey, that's the Caribbean Sea.* Then I recalled getting on a ship in Houston, heading for Panama. If I didn't know better, I'd swear I was shipwrecked somewhere in the Caribbean basin. The tall coconut trees, dense foliage, and mountains in the background reminded me of home. I wish I could remember where the ship went down. *Did I make it to Panama?*

I slowly got up, took a deep breath and looked the place over. It reeked with the smell of paradise. *Yep, I'm in Panama all right.* Noticing dusk approaching, I decided to take inventory of my body before commencing to walk. All the moving components were in working order. Pleased about that, I commenced to walk.

After a while I became conscious of my feet. Even though I was a notorious tender foot, my bare-feet didn't hurt. That raised a flag. I also realized my throat was not parched, and I wasn't hungry. Ominous signs, if you ask me. *Am I dead?* That notion raised another flag. My life's path was laden with fun and immorality, not pious behavior. *Should I be sweating a hot reception?*

After a long walk I came across a pond. I stopped to wash my face, sit for a spell and enjoy the beautiful sunset. While I was grooving, I spotted two girls peeking at me from behind a Mango tree situated on the other side. I waved at them. They waved back but remained hidden. Curious as to why they were hiding, I kept waving for them to come out.

After a few minutes they complied and came out giggling. They ran and jumped into the water. My eyes popped out. The two girls were naked. *Hey, maybe God has forgiven me, and I'm on the road to heaven.*

The girl's didn't seem to mind my presence so I removed my clothes and dove into the water. Why not? If this is paradise, I might as well taste all the goodies.

I swam towards them, hoping to get lucky. When I reached the girls my heart stopped. Not only where they beautiful, they were also young, probably in their early twenties. *God, if you're screwing with me, and this is not heaven, I'm not putting any more alms in the collection box.*

I approached the girls. "Hello, my name is Alex Perez. I'm new in town.

The girls giggled. "Hi Alex, I'm Cassandra," said the blonde.

"And I'm Becky," said the freckled face redhead."

Yes! American girls. What luck! "I'm very pleased to make both of your acquaintance," I said, trying to control an emerging urge. "Do you live far?"

"No, we live and work close by," said Cassandra. "We were going to bathe. Would you like to bathe with us?"

I pinched myself. It didn't hurt. *Damn I'm dead.*

When Becky produced a bar of soap that smelled like Sandalwood, I knew I was doomed to spend the rest of my life here. "Yes, I would love to take a bath. Can I scrub both of you?"

"Oh, yes, you can scrub us, and we can scrub you," said Becky.

A scrubbing party! Thank you, God. "Can I start first?"

"No, you are new here, that makes you our guest. We will start."

Before I could object, there were two bars of soap and several hands caressing my body.

"Ooh, Alex, you're glad to be with us," said Cassandra, as she soaped John Henry.

Glad my ass. I was ecstatic. "Don't stop soaping me," I pleaded.

Becky giggled and rubbed her breast on my chest.

At that moment John Henry decided to join the party. He drained all the blood from my brain. I did try to maintain a sense of decorum, after all this was a bathing party. Yet, when Becky slipped the bar of soap through the crack of my ass, I lost it and jumped Cassandra.

I tried frantically to find the entrance to her heavenly vaginal lips. John Henry had posture and was demanding immediate penetration. But alas, it was not to be. The girls became upset and berated me for my bad behavior. I was forced to leave the soaping party.

Hell, what did they expect? I'm a man. I have needs. Upset, but not dejected, I walked out, waved and blew kisses at them.

"Where can I find lodging?" I asked them.

"A little ways down the road you will find a place called the pearly gates. If you qualify, you can find lodging there," said Becky.

I waved once more, blew more kisses and walked away from those two glorious sets of tits.

What do they mean by, if I qualify? Mildly worried, I hoofed it, trying to get to town before darkness fell upon the land.

Before long I came to a fork in the road. *Oh, no, I hate these signs.* It's been a while, but I remembered being in front of one of these before.

Once, a long time ago, I was driving in Mexico with Ramona and her obstinate mother when we came across a fork. There were two signs before us: One read, 'God's Road.' The other, 'Pancho's Road.' I took the latter and was robbed at gunpoint by Pancho.

Since then I have learned to study the wording on signs carefully. I looked at these. One sign read, 'Road to Nowhere.' The other, 'Pearly Gates Brothel and Rum Bar.'

Well, this is certainly a dilemma. Not! I knew which one was the road to salvation, and it wasn't the one going nowhere.

I picked up the pace and soon ran into a long white stucco wall. It had broken jagged bottles on the top, and a tall black iron gate with a guardhouse in front. Next to it was a long pole with a flashing neon sign. It stated that I had arrived at the Pearly Gates Brothel and Rum Bar. *It sure looks like heaven to me.*

I walked up and knocked on the guard's door. It opened, and a handsome muscular man came out. He was wearing sexy tight Mexican Charro clothes.

"Hello," I said. "Are you Saint Peter?"

He looked at me and spat on the ground. "No, I'm not. Are you Brother John?"

I looked at the man and came to the conclusion he wasn't Saint Peter. Being a resourceful fellow, I decided to engage him in conversation.

"My name is Alex Perez, and I have come a long way to get here. Can I please enter? I have two major urges, both which can be relieved within."

He smiled. "No doubt, old chap, everyone that comes here has urges. I have some me' self, but can't get to 'em until midnight."

"Can I pass through the pearly gates?" I said.

First he frowned, and then he looked at me with disdain. He crossed his arms and bellowed. "None shall pass!"

"You can't say that."

"What do you mean I can't say that? I just said it!"

"I know you just did, but you can't use that line. I heard it in a Monty Python movie. I believe it was called "In Search of the Holy Grail." It's been used before, so you can't use it. You have to come up with a new line. Be original."

"The hell you say. I'm the gatekeeper. I can use any line I please, used or otherwise."

"I beg to differ."

"You can differ all you want, you blooming idiot. I'm the gatekeeper. I get to enforce the rules of passage."

"Are you the owner of the brothel?"

"No, I'm the bloody gate keeper. Why don't you bugger-off!"

Man, I can't believe the keeper of the gates to heaven is an obnoxious Englishman, what bad luck. Okay, here comes plan B.

"Has anyone ever told you, you look like Antonio Banderas? And that Mexican outfit you're wearing, it sure looks good on you."

He spat on the ground again. "Bugger-off. Do I look like a bloody Spaniard?"

"No, you actually look like an Englishman in tight clothes. What's with the Charro outfit? Are you trolling for *maricones*, or is it costume night at the brothel?"

He took offense at my remark and bowed on me. His eyes began to glow with anger. "Listen old chap, I'm not in the hunt for faggots. What I wear, or why I'm wearing it, is none of your business. What is your business is the fact you can't get in, so piss-off!"

"Why can't I get in, I have money?"

"Because you are not on the bloody list, that's why."

"How do you get on the list?"

"Blimey! You don't understand a bloody thing, do you?"

"All I know is Cassandra and Becky work here and I have unfinished business with both of them. How do I get into the whorehouse pal; either put me on the list or step aside. You are interfering with my needs. I want in!"

"None shall pass!"

What an idiot. Okay, here comes plan C.

"I want to get on the list, Mister Gate Keeper. How do I do it?"

He glared at me. "First of all, you have to be dead to get in. Second, you have to have done a really good deed to get on the list. In case you do not know, there are several stages to heaven. This level is reserved for those who have committed the ultimate sacrifice."

"What do you mean by the ultimate sacrifice?"

"Membership to the Pearly Gates Brothel and Rum Bar is reserved exclusively for those who sacrificed their life so someone else could keep theirs. You don't qualify, so bugger-off!"

"I know someone who qualifies, his name is John Putnam. He died so I could live. I never had the opportunity to thank him. I bet he's inside."

The man looked at the book. "Yes, Mr. Putnam is already inside, he came through two weeks ago. Nice chap, nothing like you."

"Can I get in and say hello?"

"None shall pass!"

Geez. What a moron. "Okay, you don't have to let me into the damn brothel mate. I'll just find the rum bar and have a couple of drinks."

He rushed me, grabbed me by the back of my pants and shirt, and flung me to the ground. "None shall pass, and that means you, Alex. Bugger off!"

He went back inside the guardhouse and closed the door.

As I reposed on the ground, contemplating plan D, I saw Cassandra and Becky approach the gates. Before they entered, they turned around and pulled-up their wet T-shirts giving me a good long look at those beautiful mounds with nipples.

My blood pressure shot up. I stood up and began to pound on the guard's door. "Let me in you damned Limey! Please let me in! I want to go inside!"

All of the sudden I heard a voice talking to me. *Hey, maybe it's God.* I paid closer attention. *Maybe God is going to give me a tip on how to by-pass the ornery Englishman.*

It didn't take me long to recognize the voice, it wasn't God. It was my bud, Paco Williams. "Hey Alex, wake up. You're having a bad dream."

Written during troubled times. Rated M

Walking With My Brothers

My older brother's name was Rafael, and for reasons I can't explain, he grew up with an alarming lack of morals. He was a dashing, witty, and athletic fellow. He had a certain charm with both, men and women. Throw in an insatiable desire for the female form, plus a lack of loyalty towards his friends, and you can safely say that my brother was not your average José.

It is my personal belief that God, upon realizing he had allowed passage to a devilish soul inserted another one at the last minute to neutralize the damage. By doing so, he denied them both the exclusive use of their own bodies. Alejandro was the afterthought, and his main purpose in life was to control Rafael's behavior.

You often hear individuals injected with a heavy dose of religion say that God never makes mistakes. Rubbish! Believe me, he makes plenty of mistakes. How else can we explain the presence of thieves, criminals and perverts?

If Rafael, being the first born was made in his father's image, then Alejandro, who had a mandate from God to minimize the damage his counterpart was going to unleash on his fellow humans, had to be made in his mother's image. The reasoning? If he could relate to the feelings of a woman he could deal with the task at hand. So, right from the beginning the lines were drawn, making it impossible for one to join the other. Rafael was all male, and Alejandro possessed both genes.

The ability to think clearly, to endure pain and discomfort can be said to be essential to one's survival. God loaded Alejandro with them and ensured his eventual mastery over his brother. That had to be the reason why Rafael burned the candle at both ends. He knew his tenure in the body was limited.

I'm positive Alejandro did not know, at least then, that he was going to be Rafael's assassin. Yet once he understood his role, he came to grips with it. He was not going to rush into it, instead he would pick the time and place.

Before I continue with this story, let me introduce myself: I am Salvador. By benefit of timing, I'm the youngest brother. Dad died early, and sometime after he left us Mom did too. God rest her soul. We were left, while still young in the custody of an uncle who made a living as a traveling salesman. We were left to our own devices, so we learned to cook, clean, shop, and wash and iron our clothes

At first, the relationship between my two older brothers was amiable. Rafael was in command of the body. He controlled Alejandro's time out. But as the years let-on, Alejandro's strength increased. Not only was he able to come out at will, but could stay out as long as he wanted. Then, as it is with most brothers, an unhealthy competitiveness developed, and the hatefulness began. It's safe to say the relationship deteriorated during their late teens. Rafael grudgingly gave ground to Alejandro, but started trouble on purpose, leaving his brother to face the music.

I'm telling you this because I want you to know that Alejandro took everything Rafael threw his way, and handled it as best he could. Even after he had been physically abused, he still did not complain, at least not to me.

The defense Alejandro used against his brother's onslaught was to stay out longer and longer, working on the bad image Rafael had established and nurtured.

I believe Alejandro understood and accepted the fact he was not equipped to deal with all the complexities of life. He knew he lacked certain abilities, and those were needed to deal with the aggressive behavior of the alpha males around him. Because of this, he delayed Rafael's execution. He needed his brother's toughness to handle certain matters. Unfortunately, when Alejandro finally came around to terminating Rafael, he didn't do it right, and that brought misery into my life.

This brings me to that fateful day, when a young woman named Maria Teresa came into our lives. She and Alejandro had become emotionally, but not physically involved, a situation not to her liking. I'm sure it was due to a burning desire that she talked Alejandro into switching personalities at a most inopportune time.

Maria Teresa, after touching Rafael sexually and seeing his maleness grow, became scared. She refused to continue with their tryst, and he raped her.

I want you to know that I am not defending him. This surely was a violent and hideous act perpetuated upon a daring but naïve girl. Still, I will stand on a podium and say this much: When the panties are willingly removed, a female should put out.

Maria Teresa, in a state of emotional duress did the unthinkable. She reported the incident to her priest, who then alerted the family, thus bringing her shady uncles into the fray.

"My name is not Rafael," he said to Maria Teresa's father. "I'm Alejandro."

He tried to explain the unusual situation that existed, and I must say Maria Teresa did too.

"Father," she said. "There are two personalities in that body."

But her father did not buy it. Neither did anyone else. No one was in the mood to hear such a fantastic story.

Some of the blame can be place on Alejandro's shoulders. He, wanting to impress her, explained in detail how they shared the body.

I'm also responsible. Needing to keep this innocent but provocative girl away from Rafael, I reiterated Alejandro's warning, and begged her to please beware.

"Maria," I said. "You don't want to mess around with Rafael. He does not abide by any rules except his own."

Obviously, I made him look more mysterious. She didn't listen to me either. I'm sure Maria Teresa liked the differences between them. One was a talker, the other, a doer. She must have been overjoyed to bathe in intellectual conversation with one, while playing the coquette with the other.

I tried in vain to tell her Alejandro complained to me constantly that Rafael was born with the devil within, but she would never accept him in that role.

When Alejandro tried to talk to her about his evil twin, she would laugh and chastise him. "You're nothing but a silly boy," she would tell him. "Rafael is different than most, that's all. He is misunderstood."

In retrospect, after the unfortunate incident with Maria Teresa, Alejandro should have forced Rafael out to face the accusers, especially after Maria Teresa was sent away pregnant and in total disgrace. Being a man who feared no one, he would have stood-up to her kin, and possibly made a difference in her life.

In order to save their family's honor, her revenge-minded uncles fell upon us one night after we left the Flamenco show at the Ciro Club, in Colon City.

"These guys mean business!" I told Alejandro in a state of anxiety. I begged him to change places with Rafael. "Please bring him out. He is a much better fighter, and more capable of defending us."

But no, Alejandro refused to do it. "If I do, he might win the encounter," he told me. "Rafael needs to be punished for his actions. He hurt Maria Teresa."

So he did what he had always done, which was nothing. Alejandro stood there and accepted without raising a hand in his defense the act of revenge brought on by Rafael's misdeeds.

I remember that whole scene very well. It was a humid night, being the middle of the rainy season in Panama. We took shelter under a covering in a backstreet to dodge the gully washer. We wished the rain would stop so we could continue on our way. The smell of urine in that alley was strong

It was there, while we were trying to stay dry that Maria Teresa's uncles approached us. One of them flashed a blade and shoved it into Alejandro's chest. The other struck me with his fist in the stomach, dropping me to the pavement in agony.

When I could manage, I called for help, but it was too late. Alejandro died in the ambulance on his way to Amador Guerrero Hospital.

As I rode with my dying brother, I begged him to bring Rafael out. I tried to plead, especially when I saw death at his door.

"Alejandro," I said. "Please listen to me. Rafael should be the one out here feeling the horrendous pain that comes with a knife wound."

I desperately wanted Rafael to be in control of the life Alejandro was willing to let go so easily. But he would not conjure his brother out. Alejandro thought that by dying, he would end Rafael's life. What a tragic mistake.

We buried Alejandro in Mount Hope Cemetery a few days later. This ended the family vendetta. But now, months later, I'm plagued with Rafael's presence. He did not die that day in that ambulance, Alejandro did. And now Rafael is in need of a body. He has tried to invade mine countless times, and I'm terrified that one day he will succeed.

In the grand scheme of things, the dastardly deed can be pinned on Alejandro's whimsical behavior. He started something he never intended to finish. Loose ends will snag others into matters not of their doing. Alejandro, by getting into close contact with Maria Teresa aroused in her a hormonal flame he should have doused. Instead, he ignored it, forcing her to wander from her usual familiar and safe boundaries into the arms of an immoral man.

I will close this story by telling you that the devil will tempt us, and will tease us, and then he will hide under the cover of inaction, as the situation takes on a mind of its own and goes out of control; leaving the living lost in a God-less world.

Panamanian folklore. La Tuli Vieja was the story of an old mad woman. She was professed to have had a chicken leg, and lurked in the riverbanks and cemeteries looking for children to eat. She usually appeared in the form of a crying baby. In Central America and in Mexico she was known as *La Llorona,* which translates as the 'crier.' I'm giving it to you in three parts. Rated PG

,

La Tuli Vieja

Part I

The Boogeyman of Panama

For some obscure reason, if you were eleven years or older the Tuli Vieja spared you. However, I remembered vividly being scared of her at age eleven, as I wondered how the mad old woman could tell how old I was since I did not carry an identification card with my birth date on it.

Since I'm taking some liberties with this story, let me give you the backstory behind this piece. The ominous Risacua River, which ran right next to my uncle's house and flooded on occasion was notorious for never giving up its drowned victims. This river gave me the creeps, since it was supposed to be patrolled by the spirit of the Tuli Vieja.

There were many stories about the old mad woman circulating around when I was growing up. Regrettably, most have gone to the grave with my grandparent's generation.

Recently, I flew to Panama to spend time with my mother, who had been having difficulties with her failing health. She resided in the city of David, province of Chiriquí, where the Tuli Vieja stories originated. Since I had planned to stay a while, I carried my laptop so I could continue to work on my first yet-to-be-published novel. While there, I spoke to Mother about the lack of success I had breaking into the maddening literary world, especially with a particular Hispanic publishing company in Houston.

"They have rejected everything I have sent them," I said to

her.

"What kind of stories do they specialized in?" she asked.

"The top man has an unwavering desired to acquire and preserve stories to do with our heritage. He is looking for Hispanic cultural stuff."

Mother looked at me, but became quiet. She kept on sipping her coffee, and smoking those ever-present menthol cigarettes.

I mentioned to her this particular publishing company had a reputation for its willingness to give first time Hispanic writers a helping hand. Yet, in spite of that reputation, the company had rejected all the manuscripts I had sent them.

She put out her smoke and said, "Have you sent him anything cultural?"

"Well, no," I said, with indignation. "Don't you remember that I was eighteen years old when we left for the United States? Essentially, Mother, I have been raised in Texas. I have no Mexican culture, and even though I'm still not an American citizen, I suspect the only Panamanian thing left in me is my passport. Besides, my specialty is fiction; they are looking for non-fiction."

"Let me see if I understand you, Son," she said. "They want Hispanic stories that are true, and you have been sending them Caucasian stories loaded with lies. Am I on target here?"

Knowing where this conversation was going, I tried to change the subject, but she wouldn't let me. Bela, as she is affection ally called by the grandchildren picked-up her walking stick and went into the kitchen. She asked me to help her cut the *platanos*, since it was the maid's day off.

As I sliced them into *tajadas*, she asked me if I ever heard or read the story of Mohammed and the Mountain."

"Yes, I heard it once," I said. "It had to do with a mountain that wouldn't budge."

"What did you learn from it?" She asked me.

"That he had no power. He asked the mountain to come to him, and when it didn't, he went to it."

I passed her the sliced *tajadas*. She put them in a pan full of hot olive oil and started to fry them.

In the middle of the task, she looked at me and said, "You have a lot of your father in you. Light is on but nobody's home. Mohammed had a lot of power. It was called wisdom. When something won't come your way, you go to it. Has it occurred to you to send this publisher something he is looking for?"

I bit my lip. Arguing with her has always been a losing proposition. I reminded her again that most of my friends and all of my wives had been, and still are Caucasians.

"Mother, I have no Mexican culture. My stories, although Caucasian in nature and fictional in context, are written by a Hispanic and derived from some aspects of truth. You would think the publisher would accept creative non-fiction."

She stared at me.

"If I can't elaborate on the truth, I can't write anything interesting," I said to her with conviction.

She turned her back on me and concentrated of frying the *tajadas*. After they were done, she fished them out with a fork and placed them on a plate that had a napkin on the bottom. This was done to soak up all the excess oil. A few minutes passed before she asked me if I was asking her for help, or just spouting off.

"You have an idea? I said."

"I am a female. I was born with ideas. Why don't you try and write a piece about the old mad woman of Panama."

"The Tuli Vieja?"

"Yes, that publishing company in Houston may be inclined to accept such a story. It's not Mexican, but its folklore from Panama."

After that conversation, I put my novel away and began to do some research. I became obsessed with getting something, *anything* published.

I spent the next two weeks searching for these tales by looking in the local library and asking as many old people as I dared. But information was scarce, and all those I talked with could only give me bits and pieces. No one seemed to remember what they called *Abuelita's* stories in their entirety.

This reference to *Abuelita* in itself is strange, as my grandmother, who was an avid storyteller, never told me any horrifying stories about this mad old woman. I heard them all from uncles and older male cousins.

When I was a child, we spent our summer vacation at my uncle's house in David. There was no greater terror for my brother and me than to be told, "If you don't behave, you'll be locked outside the house to spend the night on the yard hammocks."

We knew very well if we did, we would come face to face with the spirit of the Tuli Vieja, so we behaved.

Every year, as we gathered as a family in our house in Colon City to develop summer vacation plans, my younger brother and I always voted against going to David. We wanted to go and stay with our other uncle, the one who lived high up in the mountains. A place called Cerro Campana. We were hoping to be spared the trauma of living by the Risacua River and hearing these insensitive stories.

Unfortunately for us, young impressionable kids were fair game. Our mountain uncle had a story-telling son, and he harbored an indiscreet cruelty. Whenever we were left alone with him, which was every Wednesday night due to the family's love for the game of Pokeno, we were traumatized.

At night the cold wind whistled and howled around the secluded house. Our cousin, who was way older than we were, would swear the noise outside was the cry of the Tuli Vieja. He would close all the doors and windows and grab his twenty-two caliber single shot rifle.

"I need to protect you," he would say, "in case she breaks the door down and tries to grab you."

We wailed and pleaded, asking him to please make sure she didn't get inside. Then, as soon as we had calmed down, he proceeded to rev up our discomfort by telling us a particularly gruesome story.

Every child in Panama, especially those from the province of Chiriquí, sooner or later became troubled by these stories.

We were warned that if we were ever to hear an old woman or an abandoned baby crying by the Risacua, Old Chiriquí, Chagres, or any other river, we were to skedaddle out of there. In a small country crisscrossed with rivers, we never approached one without the company of at least one adult. And God forbid we ever come across a baby laying alone by the side of a river or in the cemetery.

The story I'm about to tell you is a product of my memory. It is an attempt to preserve the notorious legend of the Tuli Vieja. These stories were nothing more than fabricated lies to control spirited children by inflicting fright as a sort of discipline.

In a time when the rule, 'if you spared the rod, you spoiled the child was widely practiced, scaring kids in order to keep them from swimming the unpredictable and dangerous rivers was considered prudent. This, I'm sure, was the purpose behind the creation of such a horrible nightmarish person. Nevertheless, lies aside, we all know that folklore comes from a tinge of exaggerated truth. This one is no exception.

Part Two

The Story of the Old Mad Woman of Panama

During the beginning of the twentieth century, in a small Central American nation called Panama, there once lived a very pretty but frivolous young peasant girl named Tulia. She was half-Indian, probably from the Gnobe-Bugle tribe, and half-Spanish.

Tulia, like most girls from that era married early. By the time she was sixteen, she already had a son and a very young daughter.

Tulia's spouse worked in one of the many coffee plantations in the town of Boquete, and was often gone early and did not return until late, leaving her in the company of the children.

Tulia, whose love for her neglectful husband had waned, planned to leave the boy home alone while she and the girl went to the town of David to attend a dance in the *Toldo*, which is an area cordoned off with a bandstand built for carnival. These sites were set aside for those individuals who could not attend the clubs, or afford the dance halls.

On that fateful night, her husband was away in a neighboring village helping a cousin deliver a calf from a problem cow. As was the custom, once the potentially dangerous delivery had taken place, the rum would flow. Family members from outside the village were expected to spend the night. This encouraged her to leave the boy home, since she would be back before he woke up, and her husband returned.

It was early in the dry season. The Risacua River was running slow and stood about knee-deep to a grown man. Before she left her home and started on this ill-fated adventure, Tulia fed her four-year old boy a big meal and rocked him to sleep.

Tulia hid her party dress inside a large shoulder bag and

stepped out as if going for a short walk. She inconspicuously left the village of Dolega. When she arrived at the river, she mounted the child on her shoulders, and ventured into the water. Feeling comfortable, she proceeded to wade across. Once in it, she felt a stronger than normal current. She held on to her daughter's legs and cautiously continued her trek across.

Because the rainy season had stopped, river crossings were less dangerous now. Tulia, whose mind was focused on all the fun she was going to have at the dance, didn't feel threatened. After all, it hadn't rained on her village in over three weeks. Feeling safe, she walked across as she has done dozens of time before. It didn't take her long to sink past her knees. Tulia lifted her skirt and bag in order to tie them higher on her waist.

Unbeknown to her, many miles upriver, close to the town of Boquete, an earthen dam had broken and dumped a sizeable amount of water into the Risacua. Unexpectedly, a swell came up, causing her to momentarily loose her balance. To her horror, her child fell off. She screamed, and quickly began to reach into the murky waters trying to find and grab her child. Her efforts proved fruitless, the river had swallowed her little girl.

Tulia, frantic with fear and horror, managed to get out of the water. Then she began to run down the riverbank screaming for her daughter. People came running to her. They understood the meaning of the despondent woman's screams. But no matter how hard they tried to find the young girl's body, the Risacua refused to give it up.

The villagers formed search parties and looked extensively down river but the body was never recovered. It was this situation that pushed Tulia over the edge. Since her little girl's body never turned up, she refused to admit the child was dead, thinking that her baby girl had somehow managed to save herself.

It didn't help her mental state any that her husband publicly accused her of being a floozy and a bad mother. He blamed her, and rightly so, for the death of his daughter. After her public humiliation, he threw her out of the house. Tulia's misery increased. Her family disowned her, and her own village turned against her, casting her out.

Tulia's main concern was to find her daughter. Spouse, friends, family, and village could go to hell. Nothing else mattered to her. Exiled, she left her home with a few meager belongings and started a search that lasted for years.

Tulia began to age prematurely. This was partly due (I'm sure) to a combination of things. The first one had to be the stress of maintaining an endless vigil up and down the Risacua's banks. The second one had to be a bad diet. And the third was her constant exposure to the weather.

In the early stages of her mental torture, Tulia could be seen with a stick chasing rodents and large Iguanas (lizards) so she could eat them. She was suspected, and on many occasions accused of stealing chickens, ducks, and fruits. She was also blamed by the riverbank dwellers for missing clothes set out on outside lines to dry.

Time passed, and Tulia's countenance became grotesque. By the time she was thirty, she had lost all her teeth and had become a regular fixture at the public dumps scavenging for food and stuff. The years made her more bedraggled. Her looks became the focus of many a barbershop story, and she became fodder for newspaper cartoonists.

Every time a child disappeared, drowned, or died of a mysterious cause, the Tuli Vieja was blamed for the misfortune.

One day, a child was found dead near an area frequented by the old-mad woman. The body was disfigured in a gruesome manner and had been partially eaten, probably by a wild animal. The child's parents, distraught over their loss accused Tulia of kidnapping the boy, murdering him, and then eating his flesh. A ridiculous charge, since you need teeth to eat meat. But for some unknown reason, the *Alcalde* (Mayor) decided to act upon this ludicrous accusation, and arrested the crazy, scruffy old woman.

There was quiet talk about this injustice. Her crime was never proven. And there were people who claimed they knew the *Alcalde* had been bribed by some of the wealthy families that resided on both sides of the Risacua River to pick her up. Maybe he was bribed, but my money is on the notion he could not resist political pressure, and was forced to take action and remove this nuisance from the area.

It really was hard to blame the river dwellers. For years they had been forced to live with her incessant cries and screams. I'm sure, and understandably so, that they were annoyed and mortified at her calls for her little girl. And let's not mention what her presence did for the value of their homes. I'm sure they reached their limit of tolerance, put pressure on the mayor, and had Tulia arrested and placed in a cell.

There were those who claimed that during the time she was kept incarcerated, crime took a dip in the town of David, since no one wanted to be in the same building with her. It was also reported she kept on with her screams and horrifying wails of grief and sorrow until her death.

Tulia, once incarcerated was never released. One morning she was found hanged in her cell.

The legend grew after she passed away, reaching the level where she was depicted in drawings as having one chicken leg. This presumably a punishment since it was her desire for dancing that led her to lose her little girl.

The stories changed with the times, becoming more gruesome in nature, with purported sightings of the old-mad woman hovering in cemeteries, or crouching around riverbanks, waiting to pounce on unsuspecting children. Ultimately, Tulia became Panama's 'boogeyman.'

Part Three

A Tuli Vieja Story – "The Tragedy of Ramon"

One day, a teenage boy named Ramon was walking home from school with his two mates, Rodrigo and Juan. They had to pass by the street adjoining the cemetery, and as usual they scurried along until they reached the corner of Paradas and Molejo Street. Those two streets were the barrier between a place reputed to be full of troubled ghosts and the *taqueria* stand of Manolo Perez.

Manolo was Ramon's uncle. He owned and ran the taco stand. His wife, Maria did not work the stand, she held a job as an elementary school teacher in the nearby village of Concepcion. Working the stand with Manolo was his cousin Pedro, whose reputation for idleness was renowned. He wasn't lazy. He just loved to tell stories.

Anyone in need of quick service or peace and quiet avoided the stand when Pedro was working alone. Knowing this, Manolo tried to stay at the stand as much as possible, but there were times when he had to leave to take care of important errands.

On this particular day, and I do believe it was a Thursday because Doña Carlota, the widow of Don Norberto Venero was seen walking in the direction of the cemetery in the company of her manservant. Doña Carlota was known for her eccentricities. One of them was placing white carnations on her husband's tomb every Thursday.

Ramon's uncle left the stand to cash-in a winning twenty-five dollar lottery ticket that hit on '*El Miercolito,*' which is a mid-week lottery.

Taking this opportune moment, and being satisfied with the size of his audience, Pedro commenced to tell everyone one of his many long-winded true stories.

The *taquería* originally sat thirteen customers on stools, but Manolo, being a superstitious fellow, removed one of them when he purchased the business, thus increasing the standing room area.

The *taquería* was called '*El Palenque,*' and it sold Mexican style tacos. Yet, you could also get such Panamanian staples as *carimañolas*, fried *yuca, empanadas de carne o de fruta,* and *tamales* wrapped in Banana leaves. However, El Palenque was famous for their delicious *chichas*. The stand also had electricity, and Manolo filled your glass with lots of ice, which was a nice touch due to the warm climate.

Today, Ramon could see that one of the four large glass jars standing on the edge of the counter contained *tamarindo*. The other three appeared to be *guanabana*, guarapo, and the ever-present Mexican chicha Manolo called *horchata*, which tasted suspiciously like *Cebada*.

Ramon, eye balled the *tamarindo* jar. Developing a taste for a *carimañola*, he said goodbye to his friends and found a place in the standing area. To sit on one of the coveted stools you had to be at least eighteen years old, have gainful employment, or be a *pensionado*. If you didn't qualify, you had to stand.

El Palenque had the good fortune of being one block West of Academia Santa Maria, which is an all-girl school run by German Nuns. In order to get to the bus stop on Sabanita Street, a swarm of girls had to pass by the taco stand. The place was always packed during this particular time.

Whistling and gawking at the girls was, and still is a favorite Panamanian custom. Some of the girls, the ones with strong characters, as well as the coquettes, stopped to buy a *chicha* and stayed to talk to the dozens of boys that patronized the place.

As it turned out, Pedro was involved in telling one of the gruesome Tuli Vieja stories. And Ramon's heartthrob, Margarita Nunez was there talking with his rival, Adolfo Gutierrez. One thing led to another, and the frivolous Margarita decided to put the boys to a test. There was a dance coming up Saturday night, and she was going to bestow the prestigious first, and the suggestive last dance to whichever one of the two boys brought her a White Carnation from the tomb of Don Norberto Venero. She was going to place the flower in her hair to honor the winner. But this seemingly easy task came with a hitch. They could not pick the flower this evening, instead they had to wait until the following night, which was Friday the thirteen. And they had to do it at night and have a witness. If both boys came forward with a flower, the one who picked it the closest to midnight would win.

Margarita's cousin, Leonardo Emiliani was picked for this unenviable task. He was the captain of the school soccer team, and a boy reputed to be honest and fearless. Ramon's rival, Adolfo immediately agreed to the quest, causing him to accept the challenge.

The following day, Ramon confided to his mates a story that was already widely known, and then he asked them to accompany him to the cemetery. They agreed, setting the stage for this foolhardy adventure. And, reckless it certainly was because everyone knew the cemetery was full of disturbed spirits, and more so on Friday the thirteen. Also, to add pressure to an already difficult situation, Pedro's story at the taco stand that day had to do with a reputed sighting of the Tuli Vieja in the cemetery just a few days before. He swore that a close friend had confided in him that a man visiting the grave of a family member sometime after dusk saw the old-mad woman's spirit hovering over a tomb that belonged to a young girl who had died of mysterious causes.

This was all Ramon needed to complicate matters, another habanero pepper into an already hot *sancocho*.

The night in question arrived, and Ramon set off with his two buds for what he felt was going to be a daunting experience. They arrived at the cemetery, and to his annoyance, found a budding crowd already there. Since everyone except for the adults knew about the quest, the place was quickly filling up.

Ramon approached the cemetery gate, and checked in with Leonardo who was at the entrance. Leonardo told Ramon that Adolfo thought he had chickened out, so he went in at eleven-thirty.

Ramon looked at his watch and saw it was eleven-forty. He forced a grim smile.

To his chagrin, he was not allowed in with a flashlight, an unexpected late request by the mindless Margarita. This order, Leonardo eagerly enforced by searching Ramon and removing the Zippo and flashlight, placing it on the ground alongside Adolfo's lighter and miniature flashlight.

Ramon cursed and began to question his love for Margarita. He knew better than to do this, but his reputation was now at stake, he had no choice but to keep on walking. To compound matters, the sky was heavy with clouds, and there was a thick fog, making visibility difficult.

He continued to walk as quietly as possible, hoping to avoid running into Adolfo. He stopped his forward movement for a moment, trying to get his eyes accustomed to the darkness. When his eyes adjusted and he could actually see, he approached the area of the tomb.

Ramon was not totally without brains he had gone into the cemetery earlier that day and checked the whereabouts of the tomb. It was the one with the tall angel holding a harp. The Venero's family tomb had a black iron fence around it, and was marked by a gate with the likeness of the Virgin Mary.

After walking around a number of tombs and headstones, he finally located the angel. He stopped and checked for Adolfo's presence but did not see him. He took another few steps and all of the sudden he heard the noise of someone mumbling. He became frightened. It sounded like some sort of crying. His hair stood-up on the back of his neck and head. Ramon wanted to run away but the tomb was right in front of him.

Mustering some courage he ran toward it instead. He entered the tomb and snatched a White Carnation from a bouquet strewn on the ground. He turned quickly and started to walk away when he stepped on something that was followed by the sound of a baby crying.

Ramon turned ghostly white, and then he saw an apparition floating nearby. It was ten feet away from him and it started to come his way. Ramon realized it was the 'Tuli Vieja,' and he broke into a cold sweat and took off running, but he stumbled and fell, bruising his knees. He got up and tried to get away, but he grasped he had lost his way. Ramon kept on moving, but now panic had set in. He ran into some unexpected brambles and stumbled again. While in a frantic state, and while lying on the ground, he saw the apparition coming closer. He got up and started to run faster.

He came across another set of brambles, and, just as he was about to clear them, someone or something grabbed him from behind. With terror in his eyes he turned and came face to face with

Adolfo. His face was contorted in a gruesome manner, his eyes were filled with terror, and he was shaking but unable to talk. Ramon tried to run away, but he was caught in the brambles and could not move. He looked at the apparition and then heard a cackle.

The following morning, the police, having been alerted by the missing boys' parents, and, after questioning his close friends, entered the cemetery. They found the lifeless body of Ramon pinned to a thorn bush. His mouth and eyes were opened wide carrying an expression of horror. Next to him they found Adolfo, he was still alive but his hair had turned ghostly white, and he had lost his reason and could only babble. Both boys' were still clutching a white carnation in their hand.

Originally part of a fantasy short story collection Arcia wrote for his family. Later, the stories were reworked for the YA market, and combined into a 700 + epic novel. Lately, the stories were sorted again, expanded, and are now part of a yet to be published three book series titled, "The Adventures of the Danube Sisters." Rated G

The Wizard's Daughter

(To Sara)

A Five-Step Plan

When the birthday party for Woolsey was over and most of her guests had gone home, Soira was having a quiet supper in the dining room of the tower with Kristoff, her pirate friend. Karl, the other pirate had to take his evening meal with the hunchback in the servant's quarters.

Soira thanked Kristoff again for the wonderful gifts he brought for her, and her friends. But, she was extremely worried about the news concerning the looming arrival of the notorious Dragon Slayer.

"Why must Marika kill all the dragons? How can I stop her from doing such an evil deed?"

"She is a dragon hunter, Soira. That is what they do. They track their preys, and then they kill them. I don't know how she found out there were two dragons in Aburkia, but she did, and she's coming. I'm not sure what we can do to prevent their death, but we better do something. Maybe we can form an alliance and prepare a defensive plan."

"What kind of an alliance?"

"Who is the soldier you keep on a ball and chain?"

"He is none of your concern."

"Maybe he is, and then again, maybe he is not. What is certain, if we are to save your friends, is we need to get as much outside help as possible. If you do not mind, I want to talk to the man."

"I do mind," she said. "And we will not discuss him

135

anymore."

They finished the rest of the meal in silence. Soira's attitude about the intrusion into her private affairs left the pirate without further recourse. He decided to see what tomorrow would bring.

Soira wanted some distance between Kristoff and her imprisoned soldier, so she sent the pirate off to sleep in the servant's quarters with Hargo, and Karl.

That night, Soira was unable to sleep. She kept weighing her options, but didn't like any of them. No matter how hard she tried, she could not come up with a good solution to the problem. After tossing and turning she gave up and climbed out of bed. Maybe if she made a pot of jasmine tea and drank a cup it would sooth her frayed nerves. However, her anxiety was such that relaxing became impossible. She needed counsel, but not from Kristoff. Desperate for an answer to her problem, she opened Adrian's door and stepped inside.

"To what do I owe this late night rendezvous?" said the prisoner.

She walked over to the armchair in the corner of the room and sat. "I am in some kind of trouble, and my friend Kristoff believes you might be able to help me."

"What kind of trouble?"

"I believe my dragons are in danger of being hunted down and killed. I don't know how to stop this from happening."

He reached out to her with an open hand. "If you unchain me, I will give you my word I will not leave Aburkia until both your dragons are safe."

Soira looked at this handsome young man with mistrustful and teary eyes. Yet she felt sincerity in his voice.

"My father told me when he left me years ago that he would come back in a short time. I waited and waited for him to return, but he never did. Two years passed before I received information he had been killed in some silly war over a queen named Beatrice. If it were not for a fortunate encounter with a man who had been shipwrecked, I would have been waiting to this day for his return. It was for that reason I spared the castaway's life, since I do not trust humans. I realized the moment he told me about father's death, the importance of having access to news from the outside.'

Adrian extended his other hand to her, hoping she would

reach to him.

She got up from the chair and walked towards him. "I was left here, alone, to carry on with my life. All I had for company was Hargo, and my animal friends. The dragons and ghouls are my security, but the ghouls are unruly and undependable. The dragons are trustworthy. If they are gone, I will be defenseless against the never-ending incursions from the outside world. Besides, I love Mikee and Gabrielle very much, and don't want to see them killed."

"How about your friend, the pirate called Kristoff? How did you manage to meet a seedy character like him?"

"He is the man who told me the news about father. I gave him a bag full of gold coins that father kept in a chest under his bed. With the gold he could buy another ship, since his was at the bottom of the Sea of Uralis. In return for the gold, and for sparing his life, he promised to bring me presents, and to keep me informed on the doings of the outside world. I trust him as much as I can trust an outsider. To this day he has never lied to me, or caused my friends any harm."

Adrian brought his hands down. He realized although she was reaching out to him, she was not going to touch him.

"Listen Soira, there are two ways to save your dragons from being hunted and killed for sport. One is to tell the world they are already dead. The other is to seek and receive the protection from one of the many kingdoms in Calais."

She looked at him. Then with tears still streaking down her cheeks, she ask him, "How?"

"Soira, I'm not an ordinary soldier. I am a Prince, and I can help you with both plans, but you must trust me. If I am to accomplish the goal, I will have to leave this room."

At that very moment, Woolsey, the Wullallabe Brown bear who was spending the night, stuck his head inside the room. "I hate to interrupt this private conversation, but I have a suggestion. Anyone care to hear it?"

The following morning, Kristoff was surprised and delighted to see the soldier sitting at the breakfast table with Soira and Woolsey. After the introductions were made, and the situation thoroughly discussed, Kristoff stood-up to take his leave.

"Marika will be arriving within a couple of full moons," he

said. "I don't know if we have time to pull Woolsey's scheme off, but we can certainly try."

"We have to do it," said Adrian. "There is no other choice. His plan is the only one that can work within the time frame allowed."

"Can we stage the death of both dragons?" Soira asked.

"How can we do it?" Kristoff replied. "Marika cuts-off one ear from her victims to prove her kill."

"Would she cut the ear off even if she didn't make the kill?" Soira asked.

"Maybe no, maybe yes. Who knows for sure? But I'm willing to bet my last coin she would get close enough to the beast to see how long it has been dead, and learn what killed it," said the pirate.

Kristoff looked at Soira. "I have a plan to go along with Woolsey's, and it includes you, my dear Soira. It also includes you, Adrian. We must get started right away. How would both of you like to come see the world with a couple of seafaring men?"

It was now late in the afternoon. Kristoff and Karl had already gone back to their ship. They needed to make major adjustments to the ship's living quarters so it could accommodate the new passengers.

Soira and Adrian were enjoying a cup of tea in the garden, discussing things in general when the sorceress turned serious. "Listen to me, Adrian. In order for me to be able to let you out, I will have to be positively certain you will not run away. I can't let you leave on your word. I have little faith in man's ability to be truthful. The only way I can release you would be if we were married. Kristoff is a captain, and captains can marry people aboard their ship. He told me so, and he will do it if I ask him. Would you marry me?"

Adrian was taken aback by the unexpected proposition. He couldn't answer her straight a way, and his silence was giving the girl the wrong impression. Soira was beginning to think he didn't want her for a wife. But before he could answer her, he needed to be sure, therefore some quick soul searching was needed.

If he said yes, he would have a most uncommon wife. *What would his uncle, King Ricardo think of her?* If he said no, he was sure to remain imprisoned.

He searched for an answer. Whatever he did, it had to be the right thing. Adrian knew he loved her. At some point during his confinement, he recognized the feeling.

Beauty aside, Soira certainly was a fascinating girl. Adrian recognized he not only loved her, but he also admired her. The thought of sharing a life with her pleased him. He just wasn't sure she would fit in Tamarian society. The life of a prince's wife was demanding at best, court manners being what they were.

He knew if he married her, he would have to renounce his title, then he'd be stuck here forever. He accepted the fact she would never leave this place. *Could he be contented here?* Could he live in an uncivilized place with a surly hunchback, an eccentric wife, and a bunch of trash-talking animals?

The answer came to him. "Yes, my dearest Soira, I would be delighted to be your husband."

The process of saving the dragons was soon underway. Woolsey had six days to bring his friends to the pirate's ship. That was the first and most important step. Next, they needed to deal with the task of learning how to do animals tricks.

Woolsey was proud of himself. He had saved the day. At least he thought so. While looking at the pictures of the outside world in the book Kristoff had given him, he noticed a group of traveling minstrels doing tricks with animals in a town square. When he intruded in Adrian's and Soira's conversation the evening before, and asked the man if the slayer would kill an animal that was a trained trickster, the answer was a resounding "no." A trickster animal was trained, and therefore valuable property because they brought in money for their master.

After hearing the comment, Woolsey explained to them that all they had to do to save Mikee and Gabrielle was show up in the town where the slayer lived and do a show for her. When she saw both dragons doing tricks, she would have to stop her hunt.

They loved his conclusion, and that became the plan. Now, in order to make it work five steps were needed: The first one was to talk his friends into joining the adventure. The second step was for Kristoff to fix the ship so all of them could fit. The third was to learn tricks. The fourth was to get to Uruk without undue civil disobedience.

Woolsey understood there were to be sailors on board, as well as ghouls. He was coming with his friends, and the human hating, Magawappa-eating, Gabrielle. She was supposed to travel with them.

Kristoff told him the sea voyage to Uruk would take at least four days and nights. He wasn't sure Gabrielle could behave for that long.

The fifth step was the most difficult. They were going to do the show in a human town, and hopefully get out with their lives and freedom.

For the plan to work, the performance had to be good, and witnessed by the slayer. Woolsey wondered if they were up to the task.

The following day, after a hardy breakfast, Adrian and Soira left the tower. Hargo had to stay behind and take care of the packing, the cleaning, and the washing. Only after all the chores were completed, would he be able to join them.

Soira was busy making preparations for her wedding. She wanted to get married the day before the ship pulled anchor and sailed towards Uruk.

Woolsey had gone home to gather his friends. He walked along merrily. He felt good about things in general. He knew he had to come up with a solid plan if he was to get his friends to leave the Aburkian forest. That task was a daunting one. The thought wiped the smile off his face.

Woolsey arrived at the compound. He was greeted with the usual amiability. He went about without letting on something was up. He retired early but could not sleep. The bear spent the entire night tossing and turning, unable to come up with a way to get his argumentative friends to help him without having to call them all together for a discussion. A meeting was the last thing he wanted. His friends loved to argue, shout, and disagree. They had never left their safe world before, and had never done anything together as a group remotely resembling an adventure. Not really. This was mostly because they could not agree on anything without argument and dissention.

The Wullallabe woke up. He had a smile because he had

come up with a plan. Woolsey stretched, and rubbed the sleep from his eyes. The noise in his stomach reminded him he was hungry. He looked under the upside down bucket where he kept his extra food, but it was empty.

His stomach rumbled again. He looked around for food but there was none in the cave. Then he began to talk to himself. "What this place needs is more beehives. Yes sir, it sure would please me if there were more berry bushes around. Maybe even a field covered in sweet beets would be nice."

If words could feed you, Woolsey would never go hungry. But hungry he was, so he grabbed his hat, his walking stick, and placed the book Kristoff, the pirate had given him, along with the looking glass and stepped out of the cave. It was time to work his plan.

"What a beautiful morning," he said to himself, as he went to look for honey and berries for breakfast. Unfortunately there were none to be found close to his cave. When the illusion of a good meal faded, he realized that the only thing to eat without having to go for a long walk was cabbage.

"Ugh." He muttered under his breath. "Not again."

Author's Note

Before I can continue with this tale, I need to clarify a few things concerning the animals that dwell in the Aburkian forest. This is necessary so you, the reader, can appreciate the story better. I'll start with Woolsey. As I mentioned before, he is a Brown Bear of the Wullallabe variety. These bears have paunchy stomachs, and as a general rule are not very tall. The nature of their stomachs is probably due to the fact they are constantly eating. Wullallabes have a voracious appetite, but they are not aggressive bears. They love honey, and prefer fruits and vegetables to meat, but they can eat meat when really, really, hungry. They are not lazy, but they do love to lounge about. They are also inquisitive in nature and very intelligent. Most of the animals in the Aburkian forest avoid the Wullallabes if at all possible because their enormous curiosity, and matching appetite makes completing a task nearly impossible.

Woolsey lives with his friends in an area specially designed for them by Soira, who is known to most humans who live in the outside world as the "Wizard's Daughter." She gave her friends this particular piece of land so they could have a home, and she protected them with her magical powers.

Soira, like her late father, Marcus, guarded her territory from the intrusion of outsiders. She has no qualms about dealing harshly with those who enter Aburkia without an invitation.

Woolsey shared this safe compound with an unusual bunch of animals. The word misfits can be accurately used here, since they were of a different sort. Some were very different, others not quite so. Yet it could be said they got along fine most of the time. Well, maybe the word fine is stretching it a bit, but it can be said without fear of being called a liar that they got along as best as they could.

Woolsey has a roommate. His name is Brocko. He is a Black Bear of the Grillion type. They are tall, strong, and physically fit. Grillions like to engage in military activities. They are always marching around making noise. They are generally grumpy, stubborn, and smell awful. Their scent (or odor) comes from a diet that consists primarily of Lomba fish, cabbage, and onions. Cabbage and onions aside, Lomba is the foulest smelling fish in the world. Most animals, when encountering a Grillion, quickly move upwind.

Woolsey's other companions are: A Magawappa bull named Hoopa. An Ostrich named Sheena. A one hump Camel named Rigoberto, but since no one could roll the "R" and pronounce his name properly, they called him Rondee. Then, there is a Bald Eagle whose name is Krona. A very large Panda Bear called Baa, and two Aburkian dragons. Only the one called Mikee lives in the compound. The female, Gabrielle, has been exiled years ago for trying to eat Hoopa. Gabby is disobedient, and prefers her own company. She lives alone in a cave beneath one of the fire-spitting mountains.

It's important to know something about Magawappas. Being one is not a good thing. The human hunters, wolves, rogue bears, ghouls, and Gabrielle found them delicious. Magawappas are a special type of cattle. They have long scrawny legs, a hump on their backs, and very long sharp horns. They also possess a nasty disposition that surely comes from the fact everyone and everything is always trying to eat them. They are also short-tempered, impatient, and are always taking a dump. Magawappas are known to take as many as six dumps a day.

Hoopa's friendship with Woolsey is an oddity, since one is naturally good-natured, and the other not at all. Nevertheless, they do seem to like each other well enough, even though they are vastly different in character.

Then there is Krona, the Bald Eagle. Not much to say about her other than she was a typical eagle, always flying around. Bald eagles could be trusted, and because they are very territorial in nature, they make excellent sentries. She was wounded years ago by a human hunter's arrow. Woolsey found her and brought her to the tower were Soira's father, Marcus, attended to her wound. When she was patched-up, Marcus gave her to Soira, who sent her to live in the animal compound until she was completely healed. Krona never left. Now, let me tell you there are many who will say (in private) that she didn't leave because she had become emotionally attached to Rigoberto, the peculiar one-hump camel.

Okay, let's talk about the camel. If you look at him with a normal eye, he does appear to be ordinary, yet he is anything but average. In fact, there are many more who say he is nothing more than a walking, talking, mental case.

I have to disagree. I know better. Still, that is my belief, and I'm certainly allowed to give you my humble opinion. Yet I will agree that Rondee did have a disturbing side to him. He suffers from something we call 'an identity problem.' One he cannot resolve. Did you know Rondee was once a Dromedary? And then he became a Llama? And now, today, he is a Camel? We all know, or should know, dromedaries have one hump, and camels have two. But before I get carried away with this nonsensical dissertation about these loony animals, let me tell you the camel's story. This way, you (the reader) will be able to understand the nature of Rondee's unusual obsession and can pass judgment on his mental stability with some authority.

The Tale of Rigoberto - The One-Hump Camel

Rigoberto's parents were Dromedaries from Arabia. One fateful day, their owner sold them to a trader who took them to the province of Kashmir, in India. His mother, heavy with calf had the misfortune of being separated from her mate. She was sold to a buyer from South America. Rigoberto was born in a mountainous place called Peru.

His mother was mentally troubled. She never got over losing her mate, and failed to adapt to her new home. We have to suppose she died of a broken heart, and that type of death is a selfish one. She chose to die, and left behind a two-month old calf to face the world alone.

The young calf grew up amongst his cousins, the Llamas. He wanted to be one of them, and he tried hard to blend in with the herd, but they kept reminding him he was different. They never failed to point it out, especially when they came to a clear pool of water. They would make him look at the reflection, forcing him to notice the difference between them. Regardless of the variance, Rigoberto was a particularly bright calf, and he endeared himself to his cousins. They eventually made him an honorary Llama.

Sometime later, much to his mortification, he was sold to a man who had a good eye for special animals. This man brought Rigoberto back to India, but instead of the backwoods, he now resided in a large city called Bombay. There he became part of a herd of camels.

Though he had already been accepted as a Llama, the fact that he was not a Llama anymore confused him. Annoyed at the sudden change, Rigoberto became a private animal. He began to enjoy solitude, which is highly unusual for a herd animal.

In Bombay, he found himself living in a two-hump world. This difference caused him an enormous amount of concern, since he (again) stood out from the group.

Rigoberto's main goal in life had always been to be like everybody else, yet he was never quite able to grab on to that measure of contentment. The joy of being ordinary was never his; he was meant to be different, and that was all there was to it.

He often heard the other animals say, as they pointed at him, "Hey, there's a hump missing on that camel." Or they would say things like, "How do you put a saddle on a one-hump camel?" They would burst out in laughter as they asked him, "Do you think a human can ride a one-hump camel?"

One day, and one jest too many, he had enough Tomfoolery.

He had become a llama once, and now by the beard on his chini-chin-chin, he was going to be a camel.

He knew if he became one, no one would pay him any special attention. So, in his mind Rigoberto became a camel, and from then on he was totally oblivious to criticism.

Dromedary or camel, he was a cantankerous animal. He loved to spit, was stubborn beyond belief, antisocial, and preferred to wander the grasslands and deserts alone. Rondee, as his friends called him, was a most difficult animal to understand. He, at times, and without explanation, would go off on sojourns into the desert for days, usually returning with a bedraggled human on his back. Then, just when you were ready to give up on the notion he could be converted into a more social animal, he would surprise everyone by hanging out with Hoopa or Krona for days on end.

You would see him and the Magawappa standing side by side with their noses buried in the grass eating, dumping, and wagging their tails in total contentment. The friendship between these two had a lot to do with the fact they were four legged animals, therefore superior.

The argument here is that four legs were better than two. This view had become a source for constant debate in the animal kingdom, as the two-legged animals refused to accept it. Nonetheless, whether they like it or not, the advantage of having four legs was difficult to overlook, especially, since the criteria for being the best in the animal world was measured in terms of speed. If you were fast and carnivorous, you seldom went hungry. Conversely, if you were featured on the meat-eaters menu, but were fast, you got to live longer.

Rondee's friendship with Krona was also a peculiarity, therefore worth mentioning. Eagles by nature are solitary animals. Even so, Krona would perch on the camel's hump and keep an eye out for strangers. She was forever standing vigil over the group. The eagle would stay on the hump for hours, and neither one would say a word. Rondee would go about his daily business totally oblivious that he had this large bird of prey perched on his hump.

Then, there is Sheena, the Burundi Ostrich. She is a case unto herself. Burundis were a mysterious sort of animal, given the fact you never could find a male in a flock. Although there were hundreds of Burundis in Aburkia, they all professed to be females.

Since no one had ever met a male, and since they all looked alike, everyone was forced to accept this galling matter. Of course, there was a large group of animals who suspected the males were passing themselves as females in order to achieve the privileges afforded that gender. Yet that suspicion remained only a feeling, since no one had ever met a male.

The Burundis were pushy and self-centered. Most of the animals in the Aburkian forest disliked them because they never gave anyone a proper answer to a question, and you couldn't get them to do any heavy work.

Sheena was different from all the other Burundis. Well, she wasn't physically different, just mentally. Sheena professed she was not really an Ostrich, but an Osterreich, therefore destined to lead all Ostriches.

What is an Osterreich you say? As ridiculous as this statement may sound to you, an Osterreich is a Germanic Ostrich. To further define her claim to fame, Sheena told everyone she was of the Austrian variety. Enough said about this, no need to open a can of worms.

Mikee was a typical Aburkian dragon, tall and strong. He had a look that brought fear to all except those who knew him. Mikee had one major flaw, and as far as flaws go, his was a biggie. For a ferocious dragon, he was way too sensitive. Mikee was always getting his feelings hurt, and like Woolsey, he ate mostly fruits and vegetables. Now, we all know dragons were carnivorous by nature. That is a well-documented fact.

Mikee developed this type of diet due to the love he had for his friends, and because his sister, Gabrielle was such a voracious meat eater. In order for Gabby to be gastronomically satisfied, someone or something had to die.

Mikee, being the male of the species, was bigger and stronger, but not anywhere near as aggressive or cunning as his sister.

Gabrielle was ferocious, antisocial, and totally undisciplined. There, this about covers most of the animals in the Aburkian forest, at least the important ones. Now, if you don't mind, I would like to get back to the story.

***

Wullallabe's were not fond of cabbage, but food was food and Woolsey was hungry and too sleepy to walk far. Resigning himself, he went to the cabbage patch for breakfast. There he met Brocko.

"Hello bato," he said. "How are you feeling this morning?"

"Don't call me bato," Brocko replied.

"Isn't it a beautiful morning, Brocko?"

"Don't be so friendly," mumbled Brocko.

"As you wish my friend," said Woolsey.

He sniffed the air, and nonchalantly moved upwind. He collected six heads of cabbage and sat in the middle of the patch to eat them. When he finished, he asked Brocko if he had seen Hoopa.

"Not my day to keep-up with that ornery bull," said Brocko, in a gruff voice. "But if you happen to look in the grasslands, next to the river that has the log across it, you can probably find him. You know how Magawappas are. Always eating and dumping."

Woolsey, acknowledge the statement. He got up. It was time for him to leave.

Brocko had noticed a difference in his friend's demeanor, and decided to investigate. "How are things going with you today, Woolsey?"

"They are fine, why do you ask?"

"Because you tossed and turned all night long. You usually lie as still as a log when you sleep."

The Grillion came closer and looked at his roomy in the eye. "What could you possibly want with Hoopa this early in the morning?"

Woolsey explained that the Magawappa once told him he had discovered a shorter path that led to the coast with the high cliffs.

"Why would that information be of interest to you?"

"Because I have to be there before the moon rises again."

Brocko suspected there was more to this than his friend was letting on, especially since he was dressed for travel.

"Wait for me here," he said. "I need to get a few things,"

He soon returned, wearing his cape, steel helmet, and carrying his shoulder sack.

Woolsey smiled.

Brocko, thinking he needed to take some supplies since the

147

trip might be a long one, stopped to grab three fat Lombas from the river. He ate one and put the other two in his sack.

Woolsey was careful to remain upwind.

The trail took a turn and they left the cabbage and onion patches behind. Soon the two bears came to a field knee deep in grass. There they found the Magawappa. He had his head down, and his tail was swinging back and forth.

"Hoopa," Woolsey said. "How are you today?"

The Magawappa saw Brocko and sniffed the air; then, being as discreet as possible, he moved upwind. It was important not to insult a Grillion. If you did, you would have to fight them. And, it was not that they were such great fighters, although they were very good ones. The problem was that if you ever fought one, you would have to roll in mud and grass for days before the horrible smell wore off.

"What can I do for you today?" said the Magawappa.

"I'm in haste to get to the coast by the high cliffs, and I understand you know a faster way. I would take the main road and not bother you at all, but I need to get there quickly."

Hoopa noticed that his friends were dressed for traveling. He snorted once, and began to prance around, but before anyone could say anything he took off. "Wait here!" he yelled, as he left in a heated run.

In no time at all, the Magawappa returned with his invisible shield. This was an apparatus consisting of two pieces of mirror glass with hooks especially designed to attach to his long horns. When the sun shined on it, it would blind anyone looking down.

"If I'm traveling where man, and flying predators roam freely, I need to be very careful." he told them.

The bears nodded while looking at him in silence.

It didn't take Hoopa long to realize he hadn't been invited. Then, in an apologetic tone of voice, he told them he needed to lead them to the short path because it was too complicated to describe the way. This matter being settled, the three amigos went on their way.

Shortly, the grasslands gave way to an arid terrain. The vegetation turned to scrub brushes, sandy ground, and scrawny trees. There they came across Rondee. He was sitting on his rump, leaning against a tree with his front and hind legs crossed.

"Hello Rondee," Hoopa said.

The camel nodded and spit on the ground.

Woolsey and Brocko smiled and waved at him. He looked so comfortable they all sat on their rumps for a while, and had a nice visit. Then Baa, the large Panda showed up. She was carrying her medicine kit.

"Salutations," she said, and sat amongst them.

Not long after the arrival of Baa, Krona swooped down and joined them. Woolsey noticed she was wearing her special gloves.

The Wullallabe got up and waved his arms and bent his knees. He cleared his throat several times, indicating he was ready to continue with their walk.

Hoopa stood, snorted a couple of times and started to sniff the ground looking for his secret trail. Almost immediately he found it. Upon seeing that everyone was ready, he snorted again, pawed the ground a couple of times with his front hooves and led the way.

The harsh ground eventually gave way to beautiful fields covered in Sunflowers. While they were enjoying the enchanting view, they came across a flock of Burundis.

Hoopa, feeling frisky and needing a bit of sport, charged them.

The Burundis squealed and ran every which way. He soon tired of this, and joined his fellow travelers whom were preparing to enjoy another short rest.

Sheena approached them, panting. She wanted to know why Hoopa had behaved badly. Before the Magawappa could reply she gave him a vicious peck on the forehead. The bull howled with pain.

The blow made Hoopa mad. He jumped up, but before he could do anything about the situation, the Burundi moved behind him and pecked him fiercely on the rump. Hoopa howled in pain again.

Brocko stood up and told Sheena to stop harassing the Magawappa. He explained that Hoopa did not mean any harm by the chase. "It's just that he has four legs, and four legged creatures like to run after things."

"Please forgive me," said Hoopa. "I didn't mean any harm."

Sheena accepted his request for forgiveness. Then she noticed her friends were prepared for traveling. She asked if she could go with them. They accepted her company, and continued on their journey.

Since the group had grown considerably, Brocko demanded they all get in parade formation. After some debate and name calling, they agreed to march. Brocko borrowed Woolsey's walking stick and took the lead position. With the group placed in a tight formation of two lines of three each, they marched merrily towards the high cliffs.

Garump! Garump! One two - One two. Garump! Garump! One two. On they came, marching steadily to a cadence set forth by the Grillion.

When they finally reached the edge of the protected animal zone they stopped and contemplated the foolishness of crossing it.

The camel asked Woolsey a question. "For what reason are we leaving the safety of our compound?"

Here is my chance. Woolsey gave his friends a serious look while he scratched his cheek with a claw. "Soira is in fear for Mikee and Gabrielle's lives."

Woolsey expected this statement to be followed by the usual raucous discussion. Yet it did not come. Evidently they were caught off guard. *Hey, this is going well. Now all I need to do is bait their curiosity.* "Soira told me there was a human female called Marika, and she was a dragon hunter. She, and some of her friends were coming to hunt and kill the dragons."

They looked at each other but uttered not a word. Then they turned their gaze at him, but still did not ask any questions. They just stood there, staring.

"Soira asked me to go with her and our good friend, Kristoff, to a far-a-way land so we can stop the slayer from reaching Mikee and Gabrielle's home."

"Why did she pick you?" said the Magawappa, with a snort.

Aah, it begins. "I don't rightly know," he fibbed. "But she thinks I can be of help."

"I want to go too," said the Osterreich. "It looks like this adventure needs a good strong leader."

"Then why are you going?" countered the Magawappa.

"Count me in," Krona said. "I can be the look-out."

"Why didn't she pick me? I'm a military bear," said Brocko.

"Your smell would give us away before we could get close," retorted the camel.

"Enough talking! We will all go." Baa said, putting an end to the discussion.

That being decided, they started to march. Garump! Garump! One two - One two. Garump! Garump! One two - One two. On they came, marching in a tight military formation.

The animal troupe marched happily into what could possibly be a very exciting but dangerous adventure. They were stepping for the first time into a world that for them was full of humans, and to animals...that meant danger.

***

"Kristoff, come here quick," said Karl. "There is something you are going to find most interesting."

"What is it Karl?"

"Come and see. But hurry please."

Kristoff came over, looked and started to laugh. "I can't believe my eyes." he said.

There, coming toward his ship was a group of animals marching to a cadence set by the Black bear, who was in the lead swinging a baton. He was followed by a diverse group of God's creatures. It was hard to believe that Soira had become emotionally attached to this motley group of animals.

"This is great," said Kristoff. "I do believe this plan is going to work."

The Marriage of Soira and Adrian

Preparations for the wedding were finally completed. Everyone going in the adventure had settled into the specially designed compartments. Kristoff and Karl had worked hard, making modifications to the ship so it could accommodate all the animals.

The plan was coming along well, except the two giant perches that were built on each end of the ship were empty. Without the dragons, their efforts would come to naught. Still, Woolsey was not worried. He expected Mikee to show up soon. He knew Gabrielle would be a no-show, and he was glad. Having her along in such cramped quarters would be a terrible thing. She hated confinement, disliked humans, and had a ravenous appetite for Hoopa. She was also totally without discipline. Turning her into a trickster animal would be near to impossible.

Woolsey understood that saving both dragons might not be possible. The old animal saying that states, 'you can take dragons to water but you can't make them drink' was true. Gabrielle's unruly disposition made the task of saving her life difficult. Plus, her hatred and lack of fear for humans made her vulnerable. She would attack hunters instead of shying away from them. She was of no use to the group, at least on this particular adventure.

At dusk, to everyone's delight, Mikee appeared. He came by the ship and flew around it several times. He would fly up and then tuck his wings, shooting straight down in a fury of speed, only to open his wings at the last minute and float by the ship. Soon he tired of this and perched himself.

That evening, Woolsey was summoned to Kristoff's quarters. Prince Adrian, Karl and Soira were also present.

"I have a brother who can teach tricks to animals," said Karl. "His name is Klaus, and he lives on the great island of Malta. He once worked for a minstrel troupe and learned to teach entertaining tricks to animals."

"Well, that means we must sail directly to Malta and find Klaus," Soira said, as she grabbed a hold of Adrian's hand. "So we must marry swiftly."

The wedding was set for early evening, everyone retired to

their quarters to freshen-up.

One of the ghouls who worked as a deck hand rang the bell, signaling the time for the marriage ceremony was at hand. Soira came on deck with a crown of red roses pinned to her blonde hair. She wore a beautiful white dress.

Adrian stood next to Karl, who was holding two wedding rings. Kristoff was holding a black book. They watched with awe as Soira walked towards them.

When Adrian joined her, Kristoff asked, "Who gives this woman to this man?"

Baa gave Woolsey a sharp elbow to the ribcage.

"I do," said the Wullallabe.

The marriage ceremony took a long time, as Kristoff spoke about this, that, and other things. Some of the things said were necessary, others not entirely. Even though the animals were bored by the long ceremony, they didn't complain.

Karl handed over the rings, Kristoff pronounced them man and wife, and Adrian kissed Soira on the lips. This terminated the ceremony. They all cheered and started moving around. Everyone was in a happy mood until Adrian and Soira disappeared below decks. That signaled the end of the party.

While the married couple enjoyed a nuptial night, the rest of the group gathered on the bow of the ship and made comments about how happy the married couple seemed to be. They were all happy for Soira, and looking forward to this adventure.

The following morning Karl called everyone up on deck. He proceeded to tell them they were ready to hoist anchor and depart.

Soira refused to leave without Gabrielle, telling everyone that the whole purpose of this great adventure would be for nothing without both dragons on board.

Kristoff and Karl would not relent, telling her the tide waited for no man, woman, or dragon. They must sail out with it, and that was all there was to that.

Soira was furious. She demanded to be put back on land, immediately.

The pirates looked at Adrian for help. He cleared his throat and spoke to his wife.

"Soira, now that we are married, you must do as I say, and I say we will sail without Gabrielle."

Soira refused and demanded to be put back on land. Knowing a 'Maltan stand-off' when he saw one, Kristoff tried a different approach.

"We will be performing tricks in the kingdom of Uruk, in the town square of Mindi, in thirty-three days. That should give you plenty of time to ride Gabrielle and meet us there."

"How will Gabrielle learn to do tricks without practicing?" Asked Brocko.

"Good question," said the Magawappa. "How is she going to do tricks without learning any?"

"Don't worry about us," said Soira. "We are females, and very capable of dealing with adversity. We will be there on time, and we will have a trick or two of our own."

She kissed Adrian goodbye, and told him that to expect her to obey him was ridiculous. She was her own person and could make her own decisions. She gave Woolsey a hug, waved goodbye and climbed on Mikee who was going to give her a ride back to the tower.

That night, as they were sailing away, Woolsey reassured Adrian that his wife would indeed show-up, and on time too. He placed his big arm around the human's shoulders and asked him to walk with him.

"You need to understand your mate better," said the bear. "To expect Soira to obey you is not wise, and certainly not practical. She has been in charge of things most of her life; obeying you will never happen. If you want to have things go your way, you must side with her. If that does not appeal, you can be the leader as long as no one knows you are chief. It's called leading from behind. That's how I do it."

That being said, and hopefully understood, Woolsey left the sulking prince alone. He had other matters more important to attend to, and dealing with frail human emotions was not one of them. Adrian was going to have a hard time with Soira, and that was all there was to that.

The bear gazed out to sea and marveled at the endless mass of water. He was excited to be going away. The book Kristoff had given him had inflamed his desire for travel. He was looking forward to seeing the island of Malta, and meeting Karl's brother. He was also excited about learning to do tricks. He figured if he became good with tricks and was ever captured by humans, he could get good treatment by performing for them.

Woolsey looked at a couple of ghouls who were arguing about how to coil a long rope. Karl had been forced to instruct some of his men to teach these un-teachable creatures the work of sailors. The bear wasn't sure why Soira insisted in bringing some of these ghoulish humans along, but she did. For some reason, she wanted them to be taught the work of sailors. Woolsey yawned, stretched his arms and went below to find his sleeping quarters.

Klaus, the Trick-Master

They sailed the rough Sea of Uralis for what seemed to be a long time. Then, one morning the traveling animal troupe saw the coastline of the great island of Malta, and none too soon either. Sheena and Hoopa were both seasick.

When Kristoff dropped anchor, those able to get into the small boats rowed ashore, all others either flew towards land or jumped into the water and swam.

"We must be careful now," Karl said. "These islanders probably have never seen such a diverse group of animals. They might be frightened, especially of the dragon. I think it would be a good idea if we let Brocko lead us in a parade through the village and into town."

They mustered into formation, and soon were off and marching. Brocko was leading the way swinging the baton. Kristoff followed blowing a horn. Karl marched behind him beating on a drum. Then came the one-hump camel with the eagle perched on his hump. Behind them came Mikee, with Adrian riding on him. The Magawappa followed, marching to the rhythm of the drum. Alongside him was the crazy ostrich. Bringing up the rear was the Wullallabe and the large Panda. The ghouls and the rest of the pirates remained on board the ship.

The villagers were stunned at first, but soon became excited. They had never, ever seen such a sight before. Here in front of them, in their small and remote town was a minstrel troupe. At first, the dragon frightened them, especially when he let out a roar. But when he bowed, they lost their fear and began to clap and shout. In no time at all the whole village walked beside the travelers. They brought their musical instruments and played along with Kristoff and Karl.

The parade grew in numbers as it made it through the center of the neighboring town. There they made a turn and headed in the direction of Karl's brother's farm, which was located past the livery stable on the south side of town.

Klaus could not believe his eyes. Coming his way was a

parade. "Ingrid." he yelled, "Come quick, there is a most unusual sight coming our way."

They both prepared to greet the crowd. Klaus laughed, when he recognized Karl. The brothers ran towards each other and hugged.

Karl introduced his friends and asked his brother if the animals could occupy the barn behind the house. Klaus agreed, and Kristoff and Adrian led the animals to the huge barn where they made themselves comfortable.

Eventually, the crowd tired of the festivity, and drifted away. When everyone was gone, Ingrid brought their guests tankards of dark ale and left them alone so they could drink, talk, and smoke. Karl gave way to Kristoff, who explained to Klaus the problem facing them. Klaus understood what was expected of him. He felt he was up to the task, so he agreed to train the animals.

At the crack of dawn, the animals woke up to the sound of a loud horn.

"Who is making all that noise," said the Panda. "It can't be time to get up already, is it?"

Before they could discuss whether it was time to get up or not, Kristoff opened the barn door. "Good morning everyone. It's time to get up and pay the piper."

"I'm not paying anyone for blowing a bad horn," grumbled Brocko.

"You don't have to pay anything to anybody;" said Kristoff. "It's just a saying. It means you have to earn your keep. No one gets a free ride around here."

"Then why don't you just come out and say that, instead of trying to confuse us," said Hoopa, with indignation."

"Right," said Sheena. "What do you take us for...mind readers?"

Kristoff pondered the situation. Teaching this cantankerous bunch tricks was not going to be easy. He hoped Klaus knew how to deal with them. He decided to enlighten them in order to make things easier for everyone.

"Listen up. Please be aware that the trick-master does not understand your speech, although you comprehend his, so don't be trying to talk to him."

"How are we supposed to communicate with him?" asked

Rondee.

"The same way you did before you were able to talk to humans. I hope you understand the importance of learning as much as possible. We don't have all the time in the world. Be attentive, obedient, and practice, practice, practice."

Mumbling, and grumbling, they followed the pirate out of the barn. Then to Kristoff's chagrin, he saw Klaus standing there holding a whip and a chair. *"Oh no. This can't be good."*

"All right, you animals, line-up," Klaus said, cracking the whip.

"If he stings me with that thing, or hits me with the chair, I'll melt his skin," said Mikee. "And to show his displeasure, he roared and snorted smoke and fire.

"What's the deal with the fire breathing beast?" Klaus asked Kristoff.

"He wants you to lose the whip and the chair. He feels threatened."

"I will do no such thing," he said. "These are tools of the trade. I need them."

The ostrich came over, and without provocation gave Klaus a hard peck on his foot. The man screamed with pain. He grabbed his foot and started jumping around. Then Hoopa gave out a snort, and began to paw the ground.

Kristoff recognized the bull's mood. Yet before he could interfere, the Magawappa charged and head-butted the hapless trainer on the rump, knocking him to the ground.

The pirate placed both hands on his waist and frowned. Baa came over to him and whispered. "You told us to treat humans the old way. I don't think Klaus will survive long enough to teach anybody anything."

It took the trainer two days to recover from his first teaching attempt. He quickly learned the wisdom of losing the whip and chair, and he also changed his style.

The trick-master became exasperated countless times, and had to suffer the degradation of being pecked again by Sheena. She objected to the manner he had addressed her. Calling her "Chicken Little," was insulting. She had a brain, and she made him pay for the insinuation that she didn't.

The task of teaching this unreasonable group became

burdensome, and sometimes it felt futile. But Karl insisted the animals had to be taught to do tricks, so Klaus endured.

They didn't learn many performing tricks, just enough to get them by. Instead of each individual learning several tricks, they consoled themselves with mastering one each. The exception was Woolsey, who paid attention and did very well in trickster class. He was sorry they had run out of time. He wanted to learn more.

The goal was achieved, and that was the important thing. They thanked Klaus very much, and agreed to exit the town with a grand parade. After much ado, they packed their belongings and took their positions. With dozens of villagers participating, they proceeded to march towards their ship. The road to the coast was filled to capacity with people yelling and waving goodbye.

The animals were happy. They were glad the trick classes were finally over. Woolsey seemed content too. He was a proud bear, marching and waving a piece of paper he had requested from Klaus. The paper said, in human scribbling, that he had finished trickster school at the top of his class.

The Dragon Slayer

Kristoff and company arrived during the wee hours of the morning. They dropped anchor several leagues from the Urukian port town of Mindi. Before they disembarked, they went over the plan one more time.

First and most important was the need to remain undetected until it was necessary to show their faces. A pirate ship would certainly bring the unwanted attention of the Royal Urukian warships. Second, a thorough reconnaissance of the town had to be conducted.

Kristoff, who normally would have kept out of sight because he was a notorious pirate (and they hung pirates in Uruk) took a chance and walked out in public the following morning. He went out with the young Tamarian Prince, Adrian. It was their job to solve the logistics of their escapade.

The first matter on the agenda was to find and book a good spot in the town's square where they could perform. Then they needed to locate Marika Danube, the notorious "Dragon Slayer," and send her an invitation.

They located the magistrate in charge of Mindi, and paid a fee for a spot they felt was appropriate for the show. They made inquiries and learned where Marika could be found, and to their surprise…they were told she was now the Queen of Uruk. She lived with her husband, King Lotha Kassarov, in a castle half a day's ride away. Couriers were hired to deliver the invitation.

Tasks completed, Kristoff and Adrian decided to stop at a tavern for a tankard of dark ale. They were thirsty and didn't think about the consequences of such a move.

Unwisely, they walked into a crowded place called the Oasis Inn. When they entered, the place became eerily quiet.

As is the case in small towns, strangers were cause for suspicion and curiosity. After a few minutes the loud murmur of dozens of inquiring voices faded, filling the hall again with the usual tavern chatter. The two newcomers found a table, sat down and ordered two ales.

A large bearded man sitting at a corner table thought he recognized the pirate, so he walked to their table.

"Good day strangers," he said, tipping his cap. His left cheek began to twitch as he turned his attention to the pirate. "Pardon my intrusion, but aren't you Kristoff, the murdering scum of the earth everyone calls the "Scourge of Uralis?""

Ordinarily, Kristoff would have dealt with the insult quickly. But today he smiled, showing his gold tooth. "No, I'm afraid you have mistaken me for someone else. My name is Barnabus, and I am the owner of a traveling minstrel show."

The man hesitated for a moment. But the more he looked at Kristoff, the more convinced he became. He refused to leave him alone and continued with his harassment. He insisted, loudly that he was indeed the infamous pirate. The situation became tense. A crowd began to gather round the two strangers.

Kristoff and Adrian knew they were in trouble. When it became apparent they were going to have to fight their way out of the tavern, they stood up. Yet, before swords were drawn, a young woman's voice rang out from the far corner of the tavern.

"Leave him be or die!"

The angry man placed his hand on his sword and turned around. "Who speaks to me in this fashion? What woman dares threaten me?"

"I do," said a young girl with blonde hair.

Everyone turned to look at her. She was indeed pretty, and wore her hair pulled back from her face. She also had the demeanor of someone who was a stranger to fear.

When she got up from her chair the room became quiet again, the bar patrons held their collective breath, waiting to see who was going to make the next move.

The girl moved towards the mouthy bully. He stood his ground. A path opened, giving them ample space to settle their differences.

Adrian recognized the female's voice and turned towards it. He placed his hand on the top of his sword handle and smiled. "Hello Soira. What are you doing in a tavern?"

The stranger turned toward Adrian with a menacing stance. "Who is the young Lass who threatens me?"

Adrian smiled. "She is a dragon rider."

The man laughed and spat on the tavern floor. Then with scorn in his eyes and hatred in his voice, he bellowed: "If she's a dragon rider, I am Alexis, the Ghost that Walks the Earth."

The crowd burst into laughter.

Adrian looked at the arrogant man and spoke. "She will ride one in two days. If you dare to attend the show, she will introduce you to a dragon you will never forget."

"You are a liar," said the man.

Adrian brought his sword out swiftly. The brute did likewise. Before they could touch steel to steel, the girl extended her arm with her fingers opened and began to yell her incantation. "Shitza-dum-kriart-mar-tuzdu!"

She started to slowly close her fingers as she repeated the words. "Shitza-dum-kriart-mar-tuzdu!"

The man began to choke. He dropped his sword and gasped for air. He was on the ground writhing and turning blue when Adrian told her to stop it.

Soira released her grip, and the man began to breathe again. No one said a word. The crowd was stunned. After a moment, the murmur of the crowd began to overpower the silence again. The magical powers of the young girl had made an impression, an ominous one, but an impression nonetheless.

Kristoff took this opportunity to promote the show. He stepped on a chair and climbed on the table. "Be at the forward corner of the square for a show that will end all shows."

Then he pointed at the young girl. "See the famous "Wizard's Daughter" ride a fire-breathing Aburkian Dragon. She will mesmerize you with her magic spells and incantations. Come and bring the family, friends, and neighbors to witness a show that will amaze all. Our trained animals will do tricks never before seen. The show will open in two days, and will feature one performance only. But as shows go, this one will be spectacular. It has been especially designed for your beautiful queen." He bowed to an unresponsive crowd.

After he finished speaking, a few of the patrons came over and retrieved the troublemaking drunkard. The rest quickly left the tavern.

The barkeep, upset because all his customers had gone,

insisted they vacate his place of business before he called the guards.

***

"There seems to be some kind of commotion going on in Mindi," said the Urukian king to his wife. "Do you have any idea what is going on?"

"Not really" lied the queen. "But I bet it has something to do with the invitation we received last night."

"What invitation?"

Marika handed him the paper.

King Lotha read it out loud. "We are pleased to invite you, King Lotha, and you, Queen Marika, to a performance by an Aburkian Minstrel Troupe that will mesmerize you. The show is in Mindi, two days from today."

He placed the invitation on the corner table. "Just this morning I heard talk from the servants working in the kitchen about a dragon rider and a sorceress whose incantations produces spells. The invitation says we are going to be entertained by performing animals as well. Sounds like quite a show. Would you like to go?"

Marika laughed and looked at her husband with curiosity. "My dearest, do you think there is actually going to be a dragon in the show?"

"Of course not," he said, quickly. "I'm sure all this talk is designed to bring in a big crowd. I do believe the magician is going to create the illusion of a dragon, and that is worth a look-see. Would you like to go?"

Marika laughed again. "Surely you jest, the illusion of a dragon. I don't believe that is possible."

"Maybe not," mumbled the king. "But it bears watching. There is also a rumor going on that disturbs me a great deal. That bears checking out too."

"What rumor?"

"It appears someone has identified Kristoff, the Scourge of Uralis drinking in a tavern in Mindi. The gossip says he is connected to the show, and the dragon rider is purported to be Marcus fabled daughter. I need to go and investigate these allegations. Want to join me?"

"Yes, I'll be delighted," she said, with a slight nervous demeanor. "But if the man in question is indeed Kristoff, I hope you

163

do not plan to do him any harm. My sister likes him."

"He is a murderous pirate, Marika. We hang his lot in Uruk."

"I know dear, but you are the king here, and as such, you can make exceptions. I am asking you to leave Kristoff alone. Can you humor me?"

Lotha grabbed his chin and started massaging it, wondering whether to give in to his wife's request. "If he is indeed in Mindi, and I do pardon him, the people will surely complain. To forgive him would cause a stir amongst them. It would be unwise of me to do so. This pirate has been a thorn in everyone's side for years. Many of our merchant ships and their crews have fallen prey to his bloody hand."

"I know he has plundered and murdered, he is a pirate. That's what they do. Yet, if you imprison him, I can guarantee you my sister will be here in a fortnight. Will you deny the great Jana of Barkom a request for a pardon?"

Lotha cringed at the mention of Jana's name. He would like nothing more than to refuse her anything and everything. But he knew very well if he did, she would enlist his wife's help in a clandestine adventure, and together they would find a way of springing the pirate free. The Danube sisters had a loyalty to each other that overrode everyone, even husbands. Without agreeing or disagreeing, Lotha decided to drop the subject, at least temporarily.

Pirate problem aside, the Royals made plans to attend the show. Unbeknownst to Marika, Lotha was going to take along a company of heavy cavalry.

That night, Marika could not sleep. Everything kept swirling around in her head. She was trying to figure out the reason for Kristoff's sudden appearance. She didn't remember giving him her address, or telling him she was engaged and fixing to marry the king of Uruk.

We had a few laughs together in a Barkomian tavern. Surely I did not give him reason to follow me here. I'm sure my flirtation was minimal. *Why is he here?*

Not being able to sleep, Marika climbed out of bed and walked over to the balcony. She looked at the stars and looked for her lucky one. Her hunting trip to Aburkia was just a few weeks away, and now there were things going on that may interrupt it. Those rumors and innuendos floating around in the town of Mindi were not to her liking. She prided herself in knowing what went on in her kingdom, and the information her husband gave her this morning was old news to her. She was just playing possum. Marika had already questioned one of her ladies-in-waiting, a girl known for her natter. She was told that besides the pirate and the young mystic girl, there was another man with them, and this one looked and behaved like a man of class. Marika wondered if somehow this man could be the missing, and presumed dead, Tamarian Prince, Adrian Monaco.

The queen knew from many of the tales told by men who had been fortunate to survive their trek into Aburkia that there were at least two dragons roaming the territory. She remembered the excitement of her first kill. The dragon was named Torka, and it was known as the "Dragon of Death." The beast was given that name because it enjoyed killing humans. She shot the winged monster out of the sky with a well-placed arrow below the right wing, putting an end to the dragon's reign of terror. She vowed that day to rid the land of these hideous flying killers.

Marika suspected the timely appearance in Uruk of this minstrel troupe had a hidden purpose. "There is something rotten in Mindi," she mumbled. *Someone or something does not want me to go into the forbidden zone.*

She climbed back into bed and tried to sleep, but could not shut down her brain. She needed to get to the source of the problem. *If I have to postpone my hunting trip I will,* but the idea of having her hand forced did not please her. There had been absolutely no sightings of dragons in years. The idea of hunting bears and wild pigs didn't excite her; that was Jana's thing. She was the hunter in the family. Marika was a "Dragon Slayer," and there was a big difference in the two.

The news there were at least two Aburkian dragons alive excited her. She needed a kill to keep her slayer status alive. There was a need to enhance her legacy by adding at least one more beast to her list of kills. This was something she had set her cap out to do, and when she set her mind on doing something, she did it, regardless of the consequences. Besides, she had painstakingly put together a good team of hunters, and some were already on their way. Still, she had a strong feeling there were mystical powers working against her hunt at the moment. She understood that for now, she needed to lean in favor of caution.

She tossed and turned, unable to clear her mind of these troublesome thoughts. If Soira was indeed in Mindi, there was bound to be trouble. The girl had a reputation of being a great sorceress. Marika wondered whether she should send for Jana. Her sister's friendship with Kristoff might be helpful. In the end, she decided against the idea, preferring to wait and see how her husband was going to behave. If he blundered and locked Kristoff in a dungeon, then she would send word to Jana.

***

Show time arrived. The town was packed with spectators. The rumors floating round about pirates, dragon riders, and an enchantress brought in the curious, the bored, and the suspicious. There were men in the crowd that were armed and dangerous. If there was indeed a pirate in the show, his life was in danger.

The Royal Magistrate in charge of the town was well aware the ruling monarchs were attending the show. He hastily built a grandstand suitable to hold them and their entourage. He also placed a company of foot soldiers surrounding the king's stand. He placed the company of heavy cavalry that the king had sent ahead, in the wooded area of the park. There they would be close enough to help if needed, yet out of sight so as to not show the king's fear.

Although there existed a festive mood in town, there was also an underlying feeling that something ominous was going to happen. There were too many armed men drinking alcohol for this show to go on without a hitch. King Lotha's inability to understand the whole picture proved to be a disaster. He should have brought in at least an infantry battalion to compliment the company of heavy horses. There were over eight thousand people living in and around Mindi, and they were all there waiting for the show.

***

"Hurry up," Soira said. "Everybody is ready, and Brocko is itching to lead the parade."

"Are you not coming with us?" asked Woolsey.

"No, I will make my entrance later. Adrian tells me that all

166

good shows save the best for last. Gabrielle and I will provide the grand-finale."

They were all in formation. Brocko was in front. The black bear gave the signal, and the parade started. "Garump. Garump. One Two - One Two. On they came, marching to the beat of Karl's drum.

The crowd cheered wildly as they saw a bear leading the parade. They applauded when he began swinging his baton, and they laughed at his military tunic and war helmet.

The place was absolutely packed with spectators. There were children walking alongside the performers.

The Aburkian Minstrel Troupe made a turn toward the square, and soon the grandstand and ruling monarchs came into view.

Rondee, with Krona perched on his hump caused another round of laughter. Then came a loud "oooh" from the crowd, as they saw a strange looking bull with very long horns and a hump on its back, it was walking next to a weird looking chicken like animal with two long legs and a long skinny neck. These animals were a cause of wonderment because they were not endemic of the region.

After them came Kristoff. He was blowing a tune from his horn. As soon as he came into view, people in the crowd began to point at him. The multitude surged, and closed in on the performers. A loud whisper began, and you could discern statements from the crowd. "There he is," said someone. "There is the bloody pirate," said another.

Kristoff became aware of the danger, but ignored it. Woolsey also noticed the belligerence. To defuse it, he broke rank and began to wave to the crowd and give flowers to the children.

Behind Woolsey came a very large Panda bear. That caused another loud "ooh" from the throng. They had never seen one of those before. Baa followed Woolsey's lead and began to throw flowers to the crowd.

Bringing up the rear was a huge menacing looking dragon with a rider on its back. The presence and movement of the beast quieted the spectators. They moved away, allowing the marchers more room.

The last member of the parade was Karl, and he was beating a cadence on a drum. The crowd looked at his eye patch. The

167

murmur returned. They pointed and edged forward. By the time the parade approached the grandstand, the crowd had surrounded the performers and were beginning to show open hostility.

"Here they come!" Someone said to the king.

"It's about time. I was starting to wonder if this show was actually going to take place."

"I do not see Soira," Marika said, with disappointment, but the dragon rider is the missing Tamarian Prince, Adrian."

"King Ricardo's long-lost nephew? Are you sure?"

"Yes, I'm certain. I met him before. And the pirate blowing the horn is Kristoff. You are not going to do anything foolish, are you?"

"Are you absolutely sure he is Kristoff?"

"Yes, I met him too."

"You what?" said the king, raising an eyebrow.

"I met him before. Before we were married."

"Where does a princess get the opportunity to socialize with a pirate?"

"I had a drink with him at the Arranque tavern in Barkom once." And as soon as she uttered that stupid statement, she cringed. Lotha was a jealous man. She should have kept her mouth shut.

"You mean to tell me you were frolicking and drinking in a tavern with a murderous pirate? Are you being forward with me, or are you pulling my leg?"

She gulped. "I was there accompanying my sister. Kristoff and Jana are friends, and she wanted to see him. I went along to make sure Jana didn't run into any trouble."

Well?"

"Well what?"

"Was there any trouble?"

"Yes. You know my sister. There is always trouble when she's around."

"Pray tell me, what kind of trouble?"

"Oh, the usual type. She became involved in an argument and slammed the head of an impertinent pirate on a table, a couple of times. As a matter of fact, the man she beat-up is the same one that is beating on the drum.

"You were brawling in a tavern with pirates?"

She gulped again. "No, Jana was brawling. I was having a

drink." *Oh, God, I have to stop saying that.*

Lotha frowned, figuring there was probably more to the story than she was letting on, but for the moment he said nothing.

The parade came to a stop directly in front of the king, and then moved to the side, allowing the dragon and rider to come to the front.

Mikee and Adrian bowed their heads to the king and queen. This show of respect pleased the king immensely, and the crowd cheered vividly.

Lotha stood up and gave an eloquent speech, welcoming the performing troupe to the Kingdom of Uruk. He addressed Adrian by name, bringing a loud murmur from the crowd as they realized it was the lost Tamarian prince riding the winged beast.

Kristoff and Karl came up and also bowed, bringing a loud hiss from the crowd. Each of the animals took a turn bowing to the king, again bringing a cheer from the populace.

The show was truly outstanding. The Urukians had never seen performing animals before, at least not smart ones. Karl and Kristoff continued to play. Baa held a hoop so Krona could fly through it. Hoopa and Rondee kept doing a dance. Sheena did jumping tricks. Brocko juggled sticks, and Woolsey balanced a stick on his nose.

Everything seemed to be going fine. Everyone was having a good time. Then out of the blue, a group of drunken armed men surrounded the pirates and tried to hold them captive.

Hoopa, who was fond of Kristoff, charged and knocked down one of the thugs. Rondee charged in and spit a in a man's face, then he kicked another one on the thigh.

Brocko joined in the scuffle. He grabbed two men by their necks and knocked their heads silly.

More armed men entered the fracas. They grabbed and dragged Karl away. Kristoff struggled with two hooligans trying to wrestle him to the ground. Before Adrian could do anything, Lotha's soldiers surrounded him, pointing spears and arrows at both, him and Mikee.

Marika became upset. She screamed at her husband, "You promised me you wouldn't harm him!"

"I did no such thing," he said. "I did not promise you anything. Still, this is not my doing. I did not plan for this to happen. Someone is forcing my hand."

"Well? You are the king here, aren't you? Do something."

"I am. I'm making sure Adrian is not harmed. I want to return him to his uncle."

Marika grabbed him by the arm. "You better save Kristoff or you will regret it."

Lotha ordered his soldiers to take the pirates into custody, but this had the opposite result of what he intended. He wanted to save the pirates from harm, hoping to snatch them from the hostile crowd, but the drunken armed brutes turned on the soldiers, and a fight erupted.

There were not enough soldiers on hand to restore order. Before long, a bloody riot was in full swing. The town's square was in turmoil. The crowd began ransacking the stores.

Parents were trying to extricate their children from the danger and confusion. They wanted to get out before the king's heavy horses came galloping in, and ran over everyone.

Mikee remained calm; he had already communicated the situation to his sister and knew help was on its way. Dragons have a telekinetic power, which allows them to be in contact without speaking. Gabrielle alerted Soira, who became alarmed.

The cavalry arrived and plowed into the melee. In the middle of this confusion, a terrible roar came from the sky. Everyone stopped, no one moved. They weren't sure what had made that sound, but they knew it was nothing they wanted to deal with.

In a matter of seconds, the flying dragon was sighted. The crowd dispersed, the hoses bolted, leaving a group of hapless soldiers holding on to the two bloodied pirates.

Adrian dismounted from Mikee. He told the ruling monarchs that all hell was about to break loose upon them. He begged the king and queen to please get on Mikee so they could be saved from certain death.

Lotha hesitated for a moment, but Marika didn't. She climbed on the beast, so he followed suit.

Gabrielle came roaring in fast and furious. She spewed fire on everyone in her path. Soon the whole place was on fire.

Woolsey and Brocko rescued the two pirates from their frightened captors and spirited them away. The minstrel troupe escaped unhurt. They reached the ship, climbed on board and sailed away.

When Soira felt she had wreaked enough havoc on these ungrateful people, she ordered Gabrielle to fly her home. Mikee had sent his sister a mind message, telling her that he was taking Adrian and the King and Queen of Uruk to Soira's tower.

A Strange Occurrence

"You cannot keep us prisoner," said the king to Soira."

"I can do anything I like, Sire. This is my land, and I am mistress here."

"Actually, Lotha is right," Adrian said. "You can't keep them prisoner. Not unless you want to fight the entire continent. All the other ruling monarchs will send armies against you. Your home, your land, your friends, and your way of life will be destroyed."

"What am I supposed to do?" she said, angrily. "Let her come in and kill my dragons?"

Marika, who up to this point had kept quiet, decided to speak. "I have developed a different opinion about these animals. I don't believe I will ever kill one of them again. I want one for myself. The future lies in not killing them, but in breeding and riding them. I want to be a "Dragon Rider," just like you and Adrian."

Marika turned to her husband and batted her long eyelashes. "Can you get me a dragon to ride? I want to be known as the "Dragon Queen of Uruk.""

Lotha looked at her, then at Soira, and then at Adrian. "Will you sell me one?"

"No," said Soira. "These are my friends. They are not for sale."

The Urukian King stood up and addressed Adrian. "Your animal and your wife destroyed my town. The damage was extensive, and I am not going to mention the loss of life. I was trying to save your pirate friends from the unruly mob when she came in and wreaked havoc."

Lotha turned towards Soira. "You had no right to set Mindi aflame. You will either sell me a dragon, and at a bargain price I may add, or you will pay me for all the damages."

"I will do no such thing, Sire, and no one here can make me. Furthermore, you two will stay here until I say you can leave. You should have had better control over your subjects. You must not be much of a king."

Soira turned her anger on Marika. "And just who do you

think you are? You kill dragons for no good reason. You need to bow to me and kiss my feet. Your fate is in my hands. I know you killed Mikee and Gabrielle's mother."

"I am a queen! You cannot speak to me in this manner. Have you never been taught to show respect?"

Marika spoke to Adrian. "You are a prince in line to the throne of Tamaria. Do you plan to keep your wife in hiding forever? You certainly can't bring her to meet King Ricardo. He would disapprove of your marital choice. She does not even know how to address a king. Calling him Sire is certainly not proper."

"You take that back or I'll tell Mikee and Gabrielle you killed their mother," said Soira.

"Who was their mother?" asked the king.

"Torka was their mother," said Adrian. "Your wife killed her."

"Torka was an evil beast," said Marika. "She hunted humans. I killed her because she was keeping me from saving my mother. Marcus, the evil wizard had instructed the winged beast to kill anyone trying to free Mother."

"Marcus was my father! Don't you dare call him an evil man! I have a mind to cast a spell on you. I can make your nose and ears grow out of proportion and ruin your beauty."

"Stop it!" said Adrian, waving his hands. "Enough bickering. No one is doing anything to anyone. We need to calm down"

He addressed Soira. "Your father made several mistakes which led to his death. He started the war by snatching Marika's mother, Queen Beatrice. A warrior killed your father. Marika killed Torka, as well as Tarbok, the mad king. She did it to save her mother. You would have done the same thing."

"King Tarbok was my father," said Lotha, puffing up his chest. "Don't refer to him as a mad-man."

"You mean to tell me you married the woman who killed your father?" Said Soira, with disbelief.

Lotha gulped. "Well, yes, I did. I will confess to you that my love for her overpowered my grief. I will do anything for Marika, and that includes getting her a winged beast."

Soira burst into tears and ran off. Adrian felt bad. This was the first time he seen the girl cry.

The prince looked at Lotha. "Your Highness, I have to apologize for my brazen remark about your father, and for my wife's behavior. It is not her intent to be insulting or disagreeable, it is just that here, in Aburkia she controls things. You can say she is a queen, and as such, she has always gotten her way."

Adrian turned to Marika. "It is not wise to get a rise out of her. She is truly powerful, and unless you want to walk around with an elephant nose and ears, please be careful with your words. If you want a dragon, she is the one you have to negotiate with. She owns them. I can't help you."

***

Several weeks passed and things started to get tense. Everyone was expecting the invasion by the armies of the outside world to begin at any time.

One day, Woolsey noticed Marika petting Gabrielle. "Hummm," he mumbled. "I wonder, I wonder...."

Woolsey (being smart and curious by nature) was well aware of the predicament they were in, the plan he had so brilliantly conceived months ago had gone sour. Now everyone was in danger. Instead of saving the dragons from being hunted, the whole world was going to send soldiers to rescue the monarchs Soira had foolishly imprisoned. He needed to come up with another solution, and quickly.

Woolsey needed to think. He took a walk, and by chance found the Tamarian prince sitting on a log, whittling.

"Tell me Adrian," he said in a soft voice. "Do you really think we will be invaded? We have many armed ghouls, plus two dragons on our side. They don't have any. Won't their fierceness keep these people out?"

"Listen Woolsey, have you ever heard of the great Jana of Barkom? Do you know who she is?"

The bear shook his head in ignorance. "I have never heard of her. Is she dangerous?"

"She is the queen's sister, and the one human female no one wants to fight against."

Woolsey stared at him.

Adrian came closer and whispered, "To add to our

misfortune, Jana will be coming with Alexis, the legendary dead-warrior. Have you heard about him?"

Woolsey nodded in agreement. "That's the one they call the 'Ghost that Walks the Earth.'"

"Correcto mundo, said Adrian. "To fight him is pure folly."

"How can a dead man fight?" Asked Woolsey.

"Do you believe in spirits?" said Adrian.

"Yes, I believe in the "Phoofer-Noofer." I know he exists. He is an evil spirit."

"Well, Alexis is sort of the same thing, except he is not really dead, and he is not evil. He is a warrior that no one can kill, and he is a personal friend of Marika. He will come here with Jana, and they will do whatever it takes to rescue her."

Adrian looked around, and continued to whisper. "Did you know that Alexis and Marika were once engaged to be married?"

"It figures," said Woolsey. "A dragon killer and a ghost. What a perfect match. What happened to the union?"

"Long story. Let me just say that Lotha stole her affections, and she married him instead."

"How about the king? Besides having a bad taste in picking a mate, does he have any mean friends?"

"No," said Adrian. "The king is a schmuck. It's his wife's friends you have to worry about. They will destroy your land and kill all who oppose them."

"Humm, yes, that can be a major problem," said the bear.

Woolsey placed his paw on the man's shoulders. "Adrian, come walk with me. I have a solution to the problem. Would you like to hear it?"

"Yes, please," said the prince.

Woolsey whispered his plan.

"You really think so?" Adrian said, impressed.

"Yes, I really do. I have never seen Gabrielle take a shine to a human before. I do believe she likes her. It is certainly worth a try. Will you suggest it to Soira? It would certainly solve the present dilemma, and it will make life for Hoopa much safer."

Adrian ran over to Soira. He told her Woolsey had noticed that Gabrielle had taken a shine to Marika.

"How does Woolsey come about this conclusion?" she asked.

"When you let the Urukian queen out for her daily walk,

Woolsey has observed that Gabrielle lets Marika pet her."

"That's impossible. Gabrielle hates humans!" She said, angrily.

"Yes, I know. But apparently she likes this one. You need to ask Marika if she wants to go for a ride. Then we can see if she can mount Gabrielle."

"Why would I want to do that?"

"Because we have to let Marika and Lotha go home before the invading armies arrive. We have already discussed the catastrophic effect their presence will have upon the land. Your powers will kill many of their soldiers, but it will not deter the one they call the ghost. He can't be killed, but you can, and so can your friends."

Soira thought about it, and much to Adrian's surprise, she adhered to his advice.

The next day, Soira asked Marika if she wanted to go for a ride on a dragon.

"I would like that very much," she said.

"You do understand that in order to ride a dragon, you first have to mount it."

"Of course, I'm a clever woman," said Marika. Then she looked at the mage. "I suppose you think I'm not capable of getting on Gabrielle's back.

Soira smiled, but said nothing.

"You are so wrong, my dear girl. I'll make you a wager. If I can get on her, you have to teach me to ride. Then, once I have learned, I will challenge you to a race. If I beat you, you will sell my husband the dragon, become my friend, and allow us to go home. There is still time to stop the invasion of your homeland. I don't want to cause you any harm. I like you."

"And if you lose?"

"If I lose the race, you keep both dragons. Lotha will stop the invasion, and we go home."

Soira grinned. "It's a promise."

A Fellowship

"Goodbye Marika," Soira said.

"Goodbye King Lotha," Adrian said.

The Urukian ruling monarchs waved back and flew off on Gabrielle.

Once Soira saw that Gabrielle had indeed taken a shine to Marika, she looked upon the queen with different eyes. Teaching her to ride was actually very easy. The girl was born to ride, and seemed to have a natural talent for riding winged beasts.

When Marika and Gabrielle beat her and Mikee in the race, she put her animosity aside and accepted her as a friend.

To Adrian, this resolution was nothing short of a miracle. Gabrielle and Soira had always been openly hostile toward humans. The exception for Soira was Hargo, her personal servant, himself, and her two pirate friends. Her friendship with Marika was a godsend. It was important for Soira to have a female friend that wasn't an animal.

The whole Urukian mess was finally over, and the best part was no one had to die. The Aburkian forest did not burn, and the tower was not destroyed.

Soira was sad to see Gabrielle go, but she understood the brilliancy of the deal. She was so proud of Woolsey. The Wullallabe surely was a smart bear.

Hargo was glad the king and queen of Uruk had gone home. He was tired of waiting on them. He was also glad to be rid of the pirates. He loved it when it was just him and Soira. The fact she married Adrian didn't bother him. He had gotten to know the man well during the time he was shackled to the bed, and he was acceptable.

The hunchback waved at the animals. They were getting ready to leave. He went back inside and started to count the number of steps as he climbed to the kitchen floor. He intended to get to the bottom of the mystery if it took all his life. Just this morning he counted one hundred and twenty seven steps, and last night there were three more steps. He wondered how many there would be now?

"All right everyone," Brocko said, "It's time to go home.

Please get in line."

They all took their place. Adrian came over and gave Woolsey a scratch behind the ear, and Soira tip-toed and kissed him on his hairy cheek. They thanked him very much for all he had done. They also gave him a medal made out of gold that was attached to a ribbon. He proudly placed it around his neck.

The animals waved goodbye and started on their journey home. Garump! Garump! "One - Two. One - Two." Off they went, marching in formation with Brocko in front waving his baton. They were going home with a feeling of contentment in their hearts. They knew that all was well with their world now. They also knew Woolsey had saved the day. They weren't quite sure how he did it. But by the size of the grin the Wullallabe had on his face, and by the big shinny medal hanging on his neck, they knew he had done something very important.

Brocko, being a smart bear himself understood that his friend was probably involved in the recent departure of Gabrielle. Baa certainly knew. She always knew there was more to Woolsey than met the eye. He was a special kind of bear. Sending Gabrielle away with the king and queen of Uruk was a grand scheme.

Baa was so proud of him. Woolsey had gotten rid of two problems in one whack. The first one was blunting the invasion of their home by the armies of the outside world. The other was getting rid of an unsavory, unruly, Magawappa eating dragon.

They were marching home with a smile on their faces. Brocko was feeling feisty today so he had them going with a quick step.

Today was a good day all right. You could tell because the surly Magawappa was no longer ornery. On the contrary, Hoopa was going home with a smile in his face.

No one ever remembered having seeing Hoopa smile before. And everyone was surprised to see that he was indeed very handsome when he smiled. Mikee was happy too, even though Soira blamed him for losing the contest, and accused him of being too fat. Heck, he couldn't have won that race if Gabrielle had one wing tied behind her back. She was way faster than him, always had been. He had lost the race, but he didn't lose his sister. No, he knew where she was going, and now he had a place to visit. Soira promised him they could go see her once or twice a year.

Brocko decided it would be okay for Woolsey to call him bato, even though he didn't really like it. It was a much too familiar term, and Grillions didn't like mushy stuff.

Sheena was happy too, even though she didn't get to lead anyone anywhere. Sometimes, especially in a crowded field, you must be strong and smart enough to know when to let others take the risks.

Rondee was walking with an unusual rump wiggle. Krona, as usual, kept a watch while perched on his hump.

Baa lagged behind as always. She felt contented though. She understood there had been a change within the group. She had felt it as soon as they left the tower. A real fellowship had evolved from this adventure.

On they went, marching merrily to the cadence set forth by Brocko. "Garump! Garump! "One Two - One Two."

Written to brighten the spirits of a family member during the Christmas holiday season in a fatherless home. Rated G

The Storyteller

(To Meagan)

During the year of our Lord 2002, in a charmed village called Fetzer, living amongst a group of toy animals was Pololo, a medium-size stuffed brown cuddly bear. Even though Pololo's world was no bigger than the size of a bedroom, he had become quite a world traveler. And, as such, he was always giving advice to those in need of it, and telling stories about all the interesting and mysterious places he had visited.

Unlike Lucy, the white fluffy rabbit, or Bingo, the plastic penguin, or even Mongo, the painted wooden elephant, Pololo was the only toy ever to leave the confinement and safety of the small house they lived in.

Whenever Milly, the girl who owned the toys left the house, she took Pololo with her.

The bear knew very well what it was like to ride in a car. Yet that experience was not always to his liking. Sometimes he would be placed in the back of the car next to the rear window causing the sun to heat him up, thus fading his lush color.

Pololo once experienced the horrendous feeling of being swept away by a fast moving river current. He also suffered the humiliation of being fished out by a long pole that poked a hole in his side. Then, before Milly's mother could patch him up, he was taken outside and clipped with pins on a clothes line so he could dry in the hot sun. This treatment further eroded his good looks, making Pololo look ragged.

One day, Kiwi and Sami, the girl's dogs sneaked into the house and came into her room. Wagging their tails, the dogs looked at all the wonderful stuff in Milly's room. They set their eyes on Lucy, and attacked her.

Pololo, wanting to protect the fluffy white rabbit from the dogs, fell off the top shelf and landed on Sami's back, scaring her. For this heroic act, he was bitten severely about the arms and legs by both dogs.

When Milly returned from school she found Pololo torn and mangled. There was fluff scattered hither and thither. She became distraught and screamed with horror at such a sight.

Pololo was again patched up. But this time, since he had been ripped apart, Milly had to take him to her Aunt Beatrice's house, where the hapless bear was placed under her sewing machine and stitched up.

Although her beautiful Aunt Beatrice did a magnificent job sewing him up, Pololo's bedraggled look increased.

Yet, in spite of this condition, the toys in Milly's bedroom loved him even more. His adventures and proven toughness gave him a special stature within the group's pecking order. He was ranked higher than Kurt, the wooden nutcracker soldier. Why? Because Pololo had seen the outside world, and that gave him something to talk about.

The rest of the toys seldom left the room; most of them never left the living-room, and practically no one ever left the fence yard. So, because of that, they had very little say to each other. Pololo's stories helped immensely with the boredom of a confined life.

One afternoon, while Milly had gone to first grade, her mother came into the room. She grabbed Pololo and shoved him into a box that had some words written on it. The toys did not understand what "Salvation Army" meant. None of them could read. But they had a bad feeling over this because it was an unusual occurrence.

After this incident, Pololo was never seen again. A terrible sadness came upon the entire bedroom. And from that day on, Milly spent a lot of time crying and pouting.

***

Time passed. The days started to get dark and cold. Then an outside tree was brought into the house. Milly, her mother, older sister, and younger brother decorated it with ornaments and bright colored lights.

Even though they were only four living in the house now, Milly's insisted they hung five stockings by the chimney. Next came bright colored boxes with pretty bows, which were placed underneath the tree.

Milly regained her usual joyful disposition. They toys did too, because they knew that one night a fat man with a white beard, wearing a red suit would sneak into the house and bring them at least several new companions. They loved to hear the jolly old man say, "Ho, ho, ho!" He always said that, and he said it very loud. The fat man would open a big bag and take out things for Milly's family to play with. But most importantly, he would bring Milly lots of new toys, and that meant they would have new friends.

As expected, the fat man in the red suit came during the night. The following morning, Milly's sister woke-up early and came into her room to get her. They liked to look at all the stuff without the rest of the family around. It was a special time they shared together once a year. They would "ooh," and "aah," as they looked and touched everything. After satisfying their well-developed sense of curiosity, they, with a smile painted on their happy faces, left the room to wake up their little brother.

Then, and certainly not before, they dealt with Mama. It was important they woke her up last because she had rules. Mama always interfered with their need to self-indulge, especially on Christmas morning.

When Mom managed to get her robe on, she'd stumble into the kitchen and start to mess with things that took time. After the family had finished eating the traditional Christmas bowl of oatmeal, and were holding on to a mug of hot chocolate covered with marshmallows, they had to thank Jesus for all the presents under the tree.

This part of the Christmas ritual Milly didn't like very much. First, it took a long time to thank him. Second, she was not entirely happy with him because her daddy was no longer living with them. But she knew she had to thank him all the same. Jesus was the reason they were alive, and he was responsible for their good health. After the long Christmas prayer was said, they tore into their wrapped gifts.

Milly loved her new toys. But at the end, when all the boxes had been ripped open, a sense of melancholy sweep over her. She took her mug of hot chocolate and sat on a chair by the side window, sipping and gazing at the woods outside. A feeling of sadness had come upon her.

She didn't quite understand it. She looked at Mama, she seemed happy looking at all her things, and so was sissy and baby brother. Yet, she felt empty. Something was missing from her life.

Somehow Milly's sadness became contagious, and it soon filled the entire room. The merriment that had existed just a few minutes earlier had been replaced by an eerie silence. The whole family felt her loneliness.

She finished her hot chocolate; placed her mug in the sink, then left the living room without talking to anyone. She opened the door to her bedroom and walked inside.

A shriek came from her room. They ran to see what had caused Milly to scream. When they came into the bedroom they smiled, she was hugging a new and spiffy looking Pololo.

Unbeknown to all, Santa Claus had brought Milly a special gift. He placed it by the foot of the toy box, which is why she hadn't seen it when she woke up.

The toys were overjoyed too. Not only because they missed him, and were glad he returned, but because now he could tell them all about where he had been. They hadn't been anywhere, and because of that, no one had anything to talk about. But, to their surprise and dismay, Pololo had nothing to say....

After a while, the toys in Milly's room understood very well the reason for his silence. Pololo was brand new, he hadn't been anywhere yet therefore he had nothing to talk to them about.

Two days later, Milly came into the room and grabbed the stuffed bear and went away. This of course, made them all happy. They knew that upon his return, Pololo, being experienced once again, would surely entertain them with thrilling stories. Maybe he would talk to them about how it felt to fall off a big horse and get trampled on, or ride in a fast Go-cart up and down a dusty road.

Yes sir, from here on out life was going to be good again. They would not have to suffer anymore from the emptiness that comes to those afflicted by boredom. The bearded jolly man in the red suit didn't forget them after all. He did hear their pleas and prayers, and made their wish come true. He brought them the best gift anyone could bring into a quiet home. He gave them a 'storyteller.'

The Alex Perez stories are nothing more than a veiled attempt by Arcia to record his memories. The idea for the next novel was set. He would write about the Arcia-French Mayan Archeological Adventure Tours. He had his usual characters lined up, but he lacked another one, a new one who could interact well with Alex. One day a stranger befriended him, and this man (who became a good friend) unwittingly gave Arcia the idea for the missing character. "An Ill Wind That Blows No Good" - Alex Perez Mexican Adventures is the third of his fictional memoir series. Rated M

'In all good tales there is always a grain of truth.' - Arcia

Beau Coutellier

I was standing outside Wally World, in Metairie, selling newspaper subscriptions when a man approached me. He was sporting a broad smile, and a nice set of pearly whites. He came over to me with his hand extended.

"Hullo," he said.

I looked at him and noticed he was wearing a hat similar to mine, except his was a seaman's cap. He seemed friendly enough, so I decided to engage him.

"Hey, how's it going? Interested in a subscription to the Times Picayune?"

"No, no time to read, sorry. I'm interested in making yur acquaintance."

I checked him out. He had an engaging smile, and seemed harmless. I decided to see where this conversation would lead.

"Okay, I'll buy that, but only because we share a similar hat style. My name is Alex Perez, who may you be?"

"Beau Coutellier is my name. Yur hat is not like mine. Yur hat is taxi driver's hat. Mine is Greek sailor's cap."

"You Greek?"

"No," he said. "Yu drive a taxi?"

"Touché," I said, smiling.

He extended his hand again. "I'm happy to make yur acquaintance."

"Likewise. What can I do for you?"

"Beau wants to swap hats. I give yu mine, yu give me yours."

"Why would I want to do that? I'm fond of my hat."

"Beau likes his too. I wear yurs, yu wear mine, and we friends for life."

Hell, I can use a friend. Something about this guy touched my sense of camaraderie. Maybe it was his long unruly black hair and hollow dark eyes. Then again, it could have been his crooked hairy nose. Although he was short in stature, he appeared to be

187

much taller. I saw the two-tone platform shoes, and grinned with admiration.

"Okay Frenchie, I'll exchange hats, but only if yours fits me. And, as far as being friends for life is concerned, I'm good with it, but only if you like me."

"Listen Alex, I like yu already. Yu give me yur hat now, I come back later and we drink coffee together."

What the hell, I always wanted to own a Greek sailor's cap. "Okay Frenchie, lets swap hats."

"My name not Frenchie. My name's Beau, yu call me Beau."

"Okay, no need to get all worked-up over a name. Stop by later and you can buy me a cup of coffee."

Beau did come by later that day; and every day after that, no matter where I was working. It's funny how life comes at you. Beau needed a friend, so he picked me. When life kicked me in the teeth and a true friend was needed, one was already on the way.

A few days later, a busybody at the seedy motel where I was staying felt the need to tell the manager I was banging one of the maids. The man became incensed and told me to leave. What galled me was there were only two maids working there. Obviously I was screwing the wrong one. I bet if I had gone for the short, fat, ugly one, he would have allowed me a measure of playfulness. Instead, the guy had the audacity to put me back on the street.

Needing to find a place to live, and not wanting to move into another lice infested motel, I accepted Beau's invitation to share his home. Why not? His level of life was better than mine. I moved my meager belongings into a two bedroom, one-bath house covered with asbestos siding. His house was built in the fifties, rested on cinder blocks, and was nestled in a low-lying area full of Palmetto palms. It also came with swarming mosquitoes. The house couldn't have been bigger than one thousand square feet, but it had an outside wood deck, and that made the place seem larger.

Beau was not what you would call an educated man, at least not book wise. Yet he had a wonderful handle on street life. He was also in possession of a good heart and a benevolent disposition. Two qualities I appreciated. We became good roomies. His place was in Algiers, across the bridge from New Orleans.

One Sunday afternoon, as we were sitting on his front deck

drinking Dixie beer, swatting mosquitoes and cooking ribs, he felt obliged to enlighten me as to why Cajuns were a special breed of people.

"We work hard, and spend all de money on a gud time. We call it "Laissez Les Bon Temps Roulez.""

"Okay, I'll buy that. I'm the same way, Beau. Let the good times roll is also my life's motto."

As he rambled on about things in general, my life began to flash before my eyes. I came to the conclusion the listlessness I was suffering from was due to my present state of unhappiness. Just like the 'Nothing' on the animated film "The Never Ending Story," apathy was creeping in on me. *Why?* I was stuck in a rut. Actually, if truth be known, both of us were bored with our mundane life. The difference between us was Beau didn't know it, at least not yet.

We both hated our jobs, and neither one had a girlfriend. He worked as a dishwasher and general kitchen help at a restaurant in the Quarter. I was selling newspaper subscriptions outside Wally World, and inside supermarkets behind a red and white striped kiosk. Not being local, and not wanting to be absorbed by the culture, I began to plan my escape.

"Tell me something Beau, have you ever considered moving out of Louisiana?"

"No, but I'm willing to listen if yu have a proposition."

"I've been thinking about moving back to Texas. Would you like to come with me?"

"Beau never lived outside Lusiana. What yu have in mind?"

"I know a wealthy woman who might be willing to lend me money to open a business."

"Dis wuman yur muther?"

"No, this woman is the mother of my estranged wife."

"Yur wife, she a strange wuman?"

"No, Beau, estranged means separated. Please pay attention and stop interrupting. I have a plan, and want to know if you're interested in being part of it."

He scratched his ass. "Will plan improve my life?"

"Maybe yes, maybe no, but it will certainly be more exciting than living in this swamp land, eating rice sausages, fighting mosquitoes, and working in a crowded kitchen. What do you say? Can I interest you in moving to Texas?"

"Maybe Beau's interested. I'm just killing time here. If life ain't no worser there than here, I make change and go wid yu. Yur my friend, please tell me about de plan."

"Okay, listen up. I have a proposition for my estranged mother-in-law that may get us on easy street."

"Is muther in law strange too?"

"Yes, mother and daughter are like peas in a pod."

"Gud. I listen to yur plan."

"How would you like to help me take American tourists into the jungles of Mexico so they can explore Mayan archeological sites?"

"Yur crazier than de hatter. Why would Beau want to do dat?"

"For the sake of adventure, to make money, and to have fun at the same time. I want to cash in on the Indiana Jones frenzy."

"Listen, my friend. I love to go wid yu to Texas, but Beau no gud wid de idea of going to Mexico and work in da jungle. Thanks, but I stay here. Yu send me postcard."

I understood at that moment he had been playing me all along. Beau had no intention of leaving his home. He was a Louisiana man, and Cajuns don't move out of the state except to avoid the police.

"Okay, Beau, don't be so hasty with your decision, I don't have anything concrete yet. It's just an idea. I'm going to go back to Texas and try to put a business plan together. If it pans-out, I'll send word to you. Will you at least think about it? Traipsing round the bush in a foreign country, wearing khaki shorts and eating bread, and goat cheese can be great fun."

"Beau will think on it. Yu go work on muther in law. Beau makes no promises, but keeps mind clean."

"Fair enough, let's shake on it."

***

Two Sunday's later, while sitting on the porch swinging the fly swatter and discussing life in general, Beau asked me why I didn't have a woman. Not wanting my friend to think less of me, I told him the truth.

"I had one, but she broke it off when she found out I was

190

boning her sister."

"Yu screw da sista? Man, dats coo-yon."

"Hell, Beau, her sister was hot, and she had been bedeviling me since we first met. A man can't be blamed for falling in with temptation. A precedent has been established already."

"What yu mean?"

"Adam gave in to Eve."

"I'm cool wid dat."

"Glad to hear it. Now, I don't want you to think I'm easy because I'm not. That I was able to resist the younger sister's efforts for months was testament to my resolve at trying to be loyal."

"Did yu beg for forgiveness?"

"I tried, but her violent behavior got in the way."

"She hit yu wid a rolling pin?"

"No, she chased me out of the house with a carving knife."

"Mais, all I ken say about dat is yu is better off now."

"And why is that, exactly?"

"Because here, wid me, yu have no problems of dat nature. Here, life is gud."

"That's a matter of opinion, Beau. All we do here is sit, drink, and eat."

"And yu have a problem wid dat?"

"Yes, my waistline is beginning to suffer. When I first arrived in Louisiana I was wearing size thirty-two jeans, now I'm on thirty-four and moving up. What we need is a good adventure. Life is enjoyed best when you move around."

He got up from his rocking chair and walked over to the pit to turn the ribs over. Then he looked at me and scratched the back of his head. "Yu are right, Alex. Beau moves plenty round here, and sometimes gud things happen."

"Like what, pray tell?"

He hesitated, while scratching his balls. I could see he was trying to put words in some sort of order. When the light came on, he began to enlighten me.

"I go to da store today and got some onyons for our dinner. Because of dat action dinner will taste better. What yu do?"

"Nothing that ambitious. I did bring the beer though, and because of that we won't go thirsty. Now, can you please explain the other side of that coin?"

He speared a whole onion with his fork and handed it over to me. It was hot so I began to juggle it. He gave me a rag, and scratched his balls, again.

"Yesterday afternoon I left work early and moved round Bourbon Street. I was trying to find me some action, maybe a dice game.

"Did you find anything exciting?"

"Yes, but there was no dice involved."

"Are you telling me you found a woman?"

"Yes, and now Beau is scratching a lot. That is not a good thing."

"How much did the bug infested love action cost you?"

"Not as much as I was expecting, but more than Beau wanted to pay."

"You are a most unusual man. I'm not sure your point is clear enough to warrant a further comment, yet it does make sense in a way. You're telling me it's not how you move, but where you move. I get the point. You're telling me Mexico can be a dangerous place for you."

Beau scratched his ass. "Yes, Mexico is a gud place for Mexicans. Lusiana is a gud place for Cajuns. Where yu from?"

I thought the statement over. The answer was going to be tricky, and surely there would be an ambush on the other side. It was best to let that dog lie.

I looked at the onion he had given me and began to blow on it. When it had cooled down enough, I bit into it. The damn thing was delicious. Beau was a marvelous cook. The ribs smelled heavenly, making my stomach rumble. He handed me one.

"Beau, what do you say we don't debate any more of life's philosophies and concentrate on eating this great tasting dinner?"

"Beau's gud wid dat."

We ate to our heart's content. Afterwards, when he was washing the dishes, I began to engage him in conversation.

"Beau, if you can wash and talk, let's move on to a more amiable subject. I told you my love story, now it's your turn to tell me yours. Why did your woman leave you?"

"Ruthie left me because I'm dumber dan a box o' nails."

"That's a cop-out, you're not getting off that easy. You have to do better than that. Give me all the juicy details."

He scratched his balls. "A while back, Ruthie introduced me to one of her girlfriends. This wuman liked to brag about how she loved to fart when she got laid. One day, I was drinking beer with Ruthie and lost my head."

"What does that mean?"

"I told her I knew a girl who could fart 'La Marseillaise.'"

"No shit? She could actually toot the tune of the French National Anthem? You can't be serious?"

"Beau's serious about de farting girl all right, but he's tone deaf, maybe it wasn't La Marseillaise. Yu need to keep dat secret quiet. Beau wished he had."

"Why did you feel the need to let that cat out of the bag? And in front of Ruthie too."

"Because Beau dumber n' a box of nails."

"Well, what did she do?"

"First, she called me a cheeting basterd. Then she hit me wid her bony knuckles. Afterwards, she took her fiddle, and de bottle of grappa she kept in de cupboard and left."

"Did you beg for forgiveness?"

"No, no need to. She was no gud for me."

"And why is that?"

"Because I need a wuman dumber n' me, and dey's hard to find. Beside, precedent already started."

"I don't understand?" I said.

"Eve smarter than Adam."

"Touché. Hey, you're not dumb at all. Most men spend a lifetime before they realize they're only on top of a woman while getting laid. Okay, let's make a pact and agree to never marry a woman smarter than us,"

"I'm gud wid dat, let's do a pinkie shake."

***

Three weeks later, I took a cab to the Greyhound Bus Station. Beau met me there. I gave him a hug, and promised to see him again. He gave me a bag that contained a piece of bread, and a boudin. It was a farewell gift. I gave him thanks for the sack lunch, and bid him goodbye.

"A revoir, Alex. Yur my friend," he said.

I waved and climbed into the bus.

Our eyes met as the bus pulled out of the station. He seemed sad to see me go. Hell, I was also sorry to part with his company. Beau was easy to deal with, and his ability to enjoy life was admiring, but I was a Texan from Panama, and my life needed more than what Louisiana had to offer.

The bus slowly made its way out of New Orleans. When it reached the Atchafalaya swamp bridge, I opened the bag lunch.

I was missing him already, yet understood there were worse things in life than leaving a good friend behind.

Adiós Amigo. Que Dios te bendiga. I will see you again.

I ate the lunch, closed my eyes, and succumbed to the rhythm of the road.

This story was cut out of a dusty manuscript and inserted into the novel "In Search of High Ground" - The Amorous Antics of Alex Perez. Arcia used it as a springboard to unleash the sexual bravura of the novel. It exposes and promotes the author's obsession with the female form, and exemplifies the futility of a female's effort once she becomes the focus of a clever man. Rated R

'The difficulty of the chase is what makes the conquest a celebratory affair.' - Arcia

Nurse Miriam

She unlocked the door and walked inside. She was carrying another bedpan, third one today. I watched her as she bent over to place it under Salahadin's bed. The woman moved her body in ways that made a grown man cry. I have a weakness for nurses to begin with. There is something about a woman in a white uniform, wearing white stockings and ugly shoes that turn's me on. Nurse Miriam was a Goddess, and she knew it.

She began to change Salahadin's gauze. His bed was on my left side. While she was engaged in the task, the Algerian slipped his hand behind her waist and let if fall gently on her behind, giving her a firm squeeze.

I smiled. *Here comes trouble.*

"Now, now, monsieur, you know very well you are not allowed to touch the nurses. Be a good patient and keep your hands to yourself. You don't want me to report you to the head nurse, do you?" She smiled at him and removed his hand.

I couldn't believe it. The bitch slapped me when I pinched her hooters. The crazy Algerian managed to get in two good butt squeezes before she removed his hand. I was envious.

Miriam finished taking his vitals and moved on to the next bed, which was mine. She noticed the clipboard lying on the floor. Before she bent over to pick it up, she looked at me. Hell, I was way ahead. My eyes were closed.

She lifted her skirt and reached down without bending her knees, her usual style. I grunted with delight as her long legs came into view. She stood-up and shot me a look of disapproval.

Nurse Miriam filled every inch of her uniform. She kept the two top buttons unfastened. She had to, those puppies needed to breathe less they suffocate inside that tight dress. The woman was endowed. Her legs and big breasts made a man wince in agony. Throw in the fact she was a redhead with freckles and green eyes, and you had a woman whose beauty was beyond comparison. Yet, the crowning glory was her ass. She possessed one that would have made a Brazilian woman wail and weep with envy.

Miriam was a female specimen sent here by a cruel God for a specific purpose. She was here to test a married man's resolve, and there laid the rub. There was no way to uphold nuptial vows with her around. Not that I adhered to that notion. But if I did, I'd be in trouble. Miriam's beautiful hot body had to have been sculpted by an artist. From the fist moment I saw her, I was doomed to become her sex slave.

Physical attributes aside, the best thing about Miriam was her mental state, she loved to tease, and for those of us confined to the fifth floor of Hadassah Hospital (in Paris) she was enticing eye candy. All the other nurses were hags.

I have been here for six days now. Courtesy of two gunshots, and a failed escape attempt.

Originally I was taken to St. Etienne's Hospital. Being a Panamanian citizen, and not wanting to deal with the animosity of the French legal system, I tried to flee. Trying to get far with a pole and a liquid bottle attached to you was a stupid notion. The Surete picked me up again, and transferred me here.

I looked at Miriam as she floated through the isle. She was an 'Angel of Mercy.' To my chagrin, she tensed up as she approached my bed. *Damn the bad luck, she has her guard up.* I sat up straight and smiled.

She approached me with caution. "Are you going to behave today, Monsieur Perez, or do I have to get physical?"

"Please call me Alex. And yes, I have all the intentions of behaving. You must not think badly of me just because I am stricken by your heavenly beauty."

"Au contraire, monsieur, I do appreciate your admiration. It's your manners that offend me."

"You must realize Miriam that your beauty and physical attributes makes it difficult for a tender man, like myself, to stay within a normal range of behavior. You're a beauty without comparison. Please call me Alex, no need for formality."

"You flatter me, Monsieur Perez, but I have to question the term tender. I don't believe it applies to you."

She wrote something on the chart attached to the clipboard, and placed it back on the bed frame slot. Then she looked at me.

"I have to reach over you for a moment. Can I trust your hands to remain where they are?"

"As much as I want to bestow homage upon your lovely breasts, I will refrain from fulfilling a recurring dream. Listen to me, Miriam. You make a man want to reach higher ground. *Gees, I can't believe I used that old Jack Nicholson's line.* Regaining my composure, I continued my attack upon her resolve.

"God blessed the world when he made you. Please call me Alex. I feel a kindred bond between us."

She smiled at me. "It will take more than flattery to get inside my undies, Alex. And, please do not mistake my behavior, I do appreciate a man with lust, but I also like him to have some class. Something you do not possess."

I smiled back. She was succumbing to my charms. She had just given me the road map to her passion bowl. I tried not to show my enthusiasm.

With disguised willingness, Miriam bent her upper torso across my chest, giving me a birds-eye view of her delicious mounds.

Now, for a man with my take on life, class has always been a trading commodity. I licked my lips and buried them and my nose into her breasts.

The bitch slapped me, again.

"Monsieur Perez, you are incorrigible! I am so disappointed. You give me no recourse but to report your behavior to the head nurse. She will have to discipline you."

"Please forgive my animal behavior, Miriam. I'm just stricken by your beauty. It's not my fault I lose all sense of propriety when you get close to me. I have never felt like this before. Your beauty brings out the primal man inside of me. Please don't report me. The head nurse will isolate me, and I don't know if I can stand being away from you. I desire you more than life."

She gave me a condescending smile. "You must think me a fool, Alex."

Her words were like a sweet melody of love to my ears. The scent of her breasts had moved my passion to another level. John Henry was up and ready for action. Encouraged, I went in for the kill.

"Miriam, if you could bestow a kiss upon my face, you will

put me out of my misery. If you can do that, I promise you I will never misbehave again."

She laughed. Her facial expression told me she knew I was a liar, yet there was a glimmer in those eyes that told me she was not going to report me. Her mannerism spoke volumes about her intentions. She wanted me, bad. Hell, her nipples were giving her away. They were reaching out to me.

Nurse Miriam looked around to see if anyone was spying on her. Those locked inside the eight-bed police ward kept their eyes shut. I loved my roommates. They were on to my deal.

She bent down, pressed her breast on my chest and gave me a kiss on the cheek. Then she whispered in my ear. "Alex, you may kiss one of my breast, but only one. If you break your promise I will send you away. Which one would you like to nurture?"

"The left one," I said, gasping for air. "Please let me adore the left one."

She looked around again to make sure no one was spying on her. Satisfied, she took both of them out of their restraint and brought the left one up to my lips.

My blood pressure went right through the roof. I fought back the need to devour both. Giving me a shot at only one was sheer torture. However, I was a man on a hunt for beaver. To bag one, control was now required. I took a deep breath and deposited a gentle wet kiss on the left one.

She gasped, but did not withdraw. Her left hand gripped my arm.

My lips moved to the nipple, drawing it into my mouth. Needing to raise the flame, I brought my tongue into play. I suckled the rock hard nipple with fervor.

Her breathing intensified. She moaned ever so quietly. "That's enough, Alex, please pull your mouth away."

Not in this lifetime.

Her breast kept getting harder and harder, bringing my fever up.

She allowed me to suckle her for a moment longer. Then she slipped her right hand down to my crotch and found John Henry masquerading as a tree trunk. She grunted, and reluctantly removed her hand. When she pulled away, her face was flushed with desire.

Nurse Miriam tried to place her puppies back into their

restraint, but they were so inflamed she had to unfasten another button. She bent down and kissed me on the cheek again, and whispered, "I have the late shift tonight, Alex. At ten I will be the only nurse on duty. I will come to you when everyone is asleep, then you can fulfill your dreams with my body."

"Here? You want me to hump you, here?"

"Animals hump, Alex. Humans love each other."

"Right, sorry, please accept my apologies. You want me to caress your magnificent body, here?"

"Yes, Alex, don't tell me you find it difficult to perform in a crowd?"

"Actually, I had an audience once. It was in a hotel in Oklahoma City. I was banging this gorgeous woman with two of my buds standing outside the glass door looking through the slightly opened curtain. Kinky stuff works for me, but I have to warn you, it might get noisy. I don't know if I can love you quietly."

"Don't you worry about holding anything back Alex, I will expect to be taken to the moon. Don't disappoint me. I will give your roommates a little something extra in their evening medications to help them have a nice deep sleep."

When she left the room, my mates broke out in applause. Abdullah, the Moroccan whose bed was on my right side gave me the thumbs-up sign.

"I knew you had it in you, monsieur Alex," he said. "Looks like you won the big prize."

Flattered, I sat up and bowed to the room. For a fleeting moment, while enjoying the accolades, I became titillated by the idea of doing another public performance. I toyed with the notion of warning them about the massive sleeping-aid coming their way.

Luckily I regained my senses. I couldn't trust my roomies to be quiet and not cheer me on. Hell, Salahadin and Abdullah, with their front row seats might lose their composure and join me in the lovemaking. I could ill afford the distraction. Also, if she screamed with orgasmic delight, I couldn't trust my mates not to applaud. That would ruin my chances of going after seconds. I wanted plenty of time to enjoy Miriam's body.

Excited over the prospect of a lovemaking evening, I doused myself with a splash of cologne.

The hours dragged on. John Henry refused to settle down,

bringing forth a measure of discomfort.

Evening came and the sedative was given. The need to fornicate increased. I was anxiously expecting to see my mates engaged in heavy sleeping.

Finally, the ten o'clock hour came and the lights were turned-off.

I waited for my 'earth angel' to approach me. Soon the shadow of a female figure appeared. It slowly came my way. My perseverance was about to be rewarded.

There was no light, and that bummed me out. *I hate screwing in the dark.* I opened my arms and said, "Come to Papa."

"Hello Alex."

"Alfred! What are you doing here?"

"It's time to get out of bed and get back to work, dick-head."

"No way, I'm not going anywhere."

Then, I saw another familiar face. It was Francois. He came over and threw me a nurse uniform, a brassiere, and a nurse's hat.

"Get dressed," he said. "We have to get out of here, and fast."

"Can you guys wait a couple of hours? I'm fixing to get laid. You two can hide in the corner and watch if you like, but I'm not going anywhere until I have tasted both of Miriam's nipples."

I froze; the blade on my throat got my attention.

"Listen to me, peckerwood," said Alfred, with a low growl. "You are a married man, are you trying to tell me you have no will power? Didn't you make a vow of loyalty when you married Julia? Put the damn dress on or I will slice your dick off and stick it in your mouth. You can't stay behind and jeopardize the operation."

"I won't talk, I promise. Besides, I've been wounded. I'm in the hospital trying to get better. Don't tell me I have to get back to work already."

"Listen Alex. There is no work. You screwed up, and the boss pulled the plug on the operation. Moreover, both were clean shots. They went right through. No bone or muscle was damaged. You had more than enough time to recuperate. Put the damn uniform on."

I was hoping my roomies would wake up and call for help, but they were out cold. Miriam had done a good job medicating them. Knowing I was done for, I kissed her image goodbye and put

202

the dress and brassiere on. I looked for shoes, but they hadn't brought me any.

"Put the hat on, Alex, we have to get out of here," said Francois.

I followed my friends out of the ward. As I passed through the nurse's station, I noticed a guard, Miriam, and another nurse tied and sitting on the floor. They were blindfolded, wearing nothing but underpants. I cried as I saw those beautiful breasts winking at me. Now I knew why the uniform I was wearing looked familiar, it was hers. Alfred had on the other nurse's uniform, and Francois was wearing the guard's clothes. When I realized I was wearing Miriam's brassiere, a tingle of excitement ran through my loins.

We walked out of the hospital through a side door and headed toward a parked car. Francois climbed behind the wheel. Alfred shoved me into the back seat and followed me in.

I couldn't believe my luck. One moment I'm about to get laid by the proverbial 'Madonna of Love,' and the next I'm stuck in a car with my weird co-workers. I glared at Francois as he gunned the car engine. We drove out in silence.

We reached the outskirts of Paris. Alfred asked a Gendarme for directions. Half an hour later we arrived at a small private airstrip. There, waiting on us was my friend, Paco. He was standing next to a propeller driven place.

We climbed into the vintage machine, Alfred and Paco manned the controls, and we took off.

I took a seat and lost myself in thought. *I bungled my assignment, got shot, didn't get laid, and now I'm being spirited out of a wine and cheese country in an old plane. What else can go wrong?*

There was a loud bang, the plane shook, and Alfred and Paco passed me. They were heading for the exit door. Francois threw me a parachute.

Why me, Lord.

A short story Arcia wrote after a catamaran trip to Isla Mujeres, Mexico, with friends and relations. Needing more words to take the manuscript to the level of a novel, he inserted the piece into "An Ill Wind That Blows No Good" - Alex Perez Mexican Adventures. This novel has a particular good mix of stories written throughout the short-lived travel business Arcia had with his good friend, Les French. Rated M

'A good set of lies should never be wasted on the weak minded."-
Arcia

A Boat Trip

We were up early. I rolled my sleeping bag and helped myself to coffee and sweet bread. I wasn't too thrilled over the boat ride, mostly because I'm prone to getting seasick. When Ivan refused to refund me the passage, I succumbed to the notion that a nice boat ride, along with some snorkeling would do me a world of good.

The other paying customers arrived, and we were introduced. The head of the German family was a man named Doctor Hansel Weizenberger. The family was from Hamburg. His wife's name was Katrina, and the twenty something year old daughter was named Hanna.

"Guten Morning, Herr Perez," said the man, as he offered me his limp hand. "I'm a doctor of psychiatric medicine. What do you do for a living?"

I looked him over. The quack seemed to be in his late fifties. His Hawaiian shirt and short trousers were wrinkled. Under great stress, I forced myself to take that cold dead fish hand.

"Good to meet you, I'm an adventure tour operator from Texas. My trip is done. I'm taking a little time off and enjoying quality time with my nephew, Ivan."

He introduced me to his family, and we took our seats. The boat ride was fun, the sea was calm and the Germans were drinking a lot. It turned out my nephew's Catamaran Island Cruise came with free beer, all you could drink. Doctor Weizenberger, his wife, and I were putting the beers away. Hanna, much to my delight was sunbathing topless on the bow of the boat. To my amazement and delight, the shrink had brought a bottle of Schnapps aboard. He showed it to me with great pride, and then invited me to drink with them. It didn't take long before all three of us were sloshed.

Due to my state of inebriation, I kept ogling his daughter's beautiful breasts with impunity, a matter that disturbed the man and his wife. Ivan was doing the same, but he was the boat captain, and that position had privileges. Admiring your customer's breasts was one of them. They didn't mind him, yet kept complaining to me about my lack of decent behavior.

"Herr Perez, you must stop looking at my daughter's breasts, your behavior is making me uncomfortable," said the German man.

"Sorry, doctor," I said. "But she's the only female in the boat not wearing a top."

"So, you want me to take my top off too so you can look at my breasts?" said Katrina.

"No, I'm good with looking at Hanna's. Thank you anyway."

Obviously she didn't hear me because she began to fiddle with the back of her top.

I began to fear the apparition of old breasts. In a panic, I approached the head doctor. "Listen, Hansel. May I call you Hansel?"

"If you must, yes, you can call me Hansel."

"Okay, doctor. You ought to know I would prefer that your wife keep her top on. I rather watch your daughter's breasts. Nothing personal, you understand."

"Herr Perez, if you persist in being boorish, I will have to challenge you."

"Uncle!" yelled Ivan. "Quit antagonizing the doctor."

"Okay, please forgive my transgressions, doctor. If your wife takes her top off, I will look at her breasts too."

"Herr Perez, you make jest of me. I warn you, I have my limits."

"Uncle Alex," pleaded Ivan. "Please stop harassing the customers."

"Okay, Ivan, I'm on that. Sorry."

I turned towards the German man, placed both palms of my hands together and bowed, Indian style. "Doctor Hammerstein, please accept my apologies. I've had a terrible time with my tour. As a matter of fact, let me say that I lost my shirt, and seem to have fallen in with an unwelcomed dose of melancholy. I'll just move my body towards the stern, turn my back on your daughter and wife, and contemplate life. Is that okay?"

"Ja, Herr Perez that would be good. It would also be good if you call me by my proper name. It's Weizenberger."

I ignored him and gazed out to sea. I had to mull over my difficulties with life. As much as I hated to admit it, I had fallen from grace and was sinking into a sea of mediocrity, fast. To compound matters, I was getting uncomfortably close to being thirty six. Since there was nothing I could do about the physical aging process, I needed to do something with the mental one. No need to grow old, broke, and stupid. And, since I was a man who strongly believed in giving counsel, I decided that maybe this time I needed to get some. What better opportunity than the present.

I looked at the doctor with some interest. Maybe my problems lie with my whimsical approach to situations. I should take life more seriously. *Hell, that can't be it. I make good plans. They just fall apart.* Maybe it's the company I keep. I should try and get new friends. *No, that can't be it, either. My friends are all battle tested.* Maybe Hansel could give me some advice. I chugged my beer and approached him.

"Doctor Weizenrbagstein," I said. "May I call you doctor Weizenrbagstein?"

"No, my name is Docktor Weizenberger. Please call me by my right name."

"Okay Hansel, sorry. May I say to you that I'm terribly disappointed your wife's name is not Gretel? That would have been great."

"Don't push me, Herr Perez. I must warn you, I'm in no mood to take abuse from you."

"Uncle Alex, would you please stop arguing with my customers?"

"Okay, nephew. Sorry."

I turned towards the head shrink. "Maybe you can give me some advice, Herr Docktor. I have a problem that's been dogging me for quite some time. Can I lie down on the hard bench and talk to you? What do you say?"

"Herr Perez, I'm on vacation, please do not bother me."

"Please do it, Hans," said Katrina. "He can rest his head on my lap, I don't mind. Maybe afterward he will leave us alone."

"If you insist, Katrina. But I must warn you, Herr Perez, if you continue to misbehave I will have to fight you. If you are serious and forthcoming with me, I will try and get to ze bottom of your problem. Am I to understand you're having sexual problems, ja?"

I stared at the man and wondered whether this impromptu session was a good idea.

"Don't be shy," he said, "I have them too, but today we will talk about yours. Can you tell me why you...."

"I don't have any sexual problems, doctor," I said, rather putout at the assumption. "That's not the reason why I'm laying my head on your wife's lap, looking at the bottom of her breasts."

"Ja, ja, I'm sure you don't. Nobody does, but I know better. You are a Hispanic man, are you not?"

"Been one all my life."

"Ha! See, I am on target," said the inebriated shrink. "Now, tell me about it. I'm listening. I bet your machismo makes it difficult to let ze woman get on top, ja? I am correct, am I not?"

I looked at the man with disdain. Yet before I could reply, Katrina motioned for me to remove my head from her lap. She stood up and filled our short glasses half full of schnapps. Hansel raised his glass and said, "Prost."

We shot them down. Katrina retrieved the glasses and put them away into her satchel. I checked out the old tits, they were getting younger by the minute. I had to fight the urge to pinch them. When she turned her back to him, the shrink walked over and grabbed a handful of butt with both hands.

"You Dum Kopf swine!" she yelled. "You need to behave. You are setting a bad example for Herr Perez. Next thing you know he will want to grab my behind too."

"She's right Dr. Wiemereiner," I said. "You're entirely too old not to know how to grab a woman's ass. I'm disappointed. I'm tempted to show you how it's done?"

"I'm not a dog, Herr Perez. My name is Weizenberger. Please call me by my proper name. And don't you tell me how to grab an ass. I am a German man, not some Latin American man who thinks patting or pinching an ass constitutes a love act. And furthermore believes that letting his woman get on top is an admittance of sexual weakness. What's ze matter, you afraid of losing control of ze love making, is that it?"

"Listen to me, doctor Wemerstein, you need to stop making assumptions. My problems are not due to sexual pride. Instead, I'm overburdened with too much temptation, and have a historical bad handle on it. Get the drift?"

"Ja, I understand very well. Your wife left you because you're a putz, and now you are trying to ruin my Caribbean vacation."

I ignored the ignoramus and continued to admire his daughter's firm breasts while I collected my thoughts. When ready, I resumed my intrusion.

"Doctor Weizenbagel, let me tell you that Ramona, my present wife is leaving me for non-sexual reasons. And, with the risk of injuring your sense of high-mindedness, let me divulge to you that she enjoyed getting on top, and I insisted on it. When in bed with a sexually ravenous female, it's best to be on the receiving end. Put that bit of knowledge in your pipe and smoke it."

"I do not smoke, Herr Perez."

"Too bad, tobacco is delightful. Still, vices are a personal matter. Don't let me brag about mine. Can we continue with our session?"

"Only if you insist," said the doctor, frowning.

"Good. Thank you. I'm in the process of getting a divorce, and the deed should be done by the time I get back to Texas. My problem lies with the fact that women like to marry me, but not for very long. I'm about to get hitched again soon to a woman I barely know."

"Herr Perez, would you please put your head back on my lap again," said Katrina. "I would like to ask you a personal question if you don't mind."

"Not at all," I said, as I buried my head in her lap. "Please fire away."

She started to stroke my forehead. "Are you a rich man or are you hanging a long one?"

"No, neither one. I'm struggling financially, and don't have more than six inches tucked in my shorts. What I do have is a good instruction book on how to make love outside, standing up."

"You must loan it to Hansel, he could use some instructions. He never makes love to me outside, standing up. With him it's always inside, laying down with the door closed"

"Katrina, please be quiet, I'm ze doctor. I'm in charge here. Don't embarrass me. Herr Perez, are these women who want to marry you, rich?"

"Yes, they are," I replied.

"I can see why women want to marry you," said Katrina, as she continued to stroke my forehead and hair. "You have a 'lost boy' look mixed with a sexual bravado that is enticing. I just met you, and I already want you cuddle you and rub your hair."

"Katrina, stop your wild behavior this instant!" said Hansel. "Herr Perez is suffering from too much female affection. He needs my advice, not your attention."

"So, you think you can help me?" I said.

"Of course I can. I'm ze doktor."

"Well?"

"Well what?"

"My problem. You are supposed to help me with it."

"Oh, yes, that's right. Listen to me, Herr Perez. I know ze root of ze problem, but don't know ze reason why you are complaining. You have rich women chasing after you. I should be so lucky. You have married women wanting to stroke your hair in front of their husbands. I should be so lucky. If you want women to stop handling you, and marrying you, you must treat them bad. You could also try saying no. Ever thought of that?"

"You want me to tell rich women to go away, is that it? Is that your professional advice?"

"As ridiculous as it may sound to you, Herr Perez, yes, I want you to say no to them. And, if you don't like my advice you can quit bothering me on my vacation."

He turned his back to me for a moment. Then with a sigh, he looked back at me. "You know what you are, Herr Perez?"

"No, lay it on me, and don't spare me the punch line."

"You are what we, in our profession call a schmuck. I wish I had your problems."

"Listen Doctor Wimerstachner, you're not helping me here."

"Stop mispronouncing my name, please." he said with clenched fists.

"Hansel, behave yourself," said Katrina. "Herr Perez is only being friendly."

The German man placed his fists on his hips and stared at me. "What do you want me to tell you? You want me to say you are a fortunate man? Is that it? You seem to know how to play tickle ze monkey's mustache very well? You know, Katrina is right, I need lessons. I don't even remember how to spank the monkey anymore. It's been years since I last saw it."

"You dumkopf swine," yelled the woman. "Don't be telling

Herr Perez about our sex life. You are giving him ideas. Next thing you know he will want to feed my monkey."

"No thank you, madam. I'm on my nephew's boat, and if you take your pants off, it will upset him."

"Herr Perez, you are a despicable man. I give you free advice, and you pay me by insulting my wife?"

"Stop it!" yelled Ivan. "I'm the captain here, and no one is taking off their pants in my catamaran. Uncle Alex, you stay on that corner. Doctor Weizenberger, you and your wife stay on the other. Do not talk to each other anymore, understand?"

We did as we were told. And believe it or not, as drunk as I was, Hansel's professional advice hit home. He was right; I needed to stop complaining about my good prosperity. If my destiny was to be up to my ass in rich young wives, so be it. I mentally thanked the shrink and his sexually starved wife, and made a promise to leave them alone.

The rest of the trip was uneventful. The Germans kept their distance, and Hanna put her top back on. Ivan threw the anchor and we stopped for a little snorkeling in the crystal clear Caribbean Sea. I followed little fishes around, and made a rational note to go home quickly and prime Julia's pump. No need to let her emotions cool down.

We had a nice amiable farewell lunch in an outdoor restaurant in Isla Mujeres. We said goodbye to the German family. They were visibly glad to be rid of me.

Screw them. This is Latin America, not Europe. We have a different sense of humor here. However, as we pulled anchor, I noticed an amorous behavior between the couple. They were laughing and holding hands. I felt good. Maybe we managed to get something out of the trip after all, besides this sunburn.

The return trip was enjoyable. The sea remained calm and I was able to take a snooze. We made it back to Cancun, I said goodbye to Ivan. He seemed glad to see me leave. Then, with lean pockets, and a good new perspective on life, I bought a bus ticket and rode it all the way to the Texas border.

About the Author

Alberto Arcia was born in the province of Colon, in the Republic of Panama. He began to write in earnest during his forties. At that time he wrote mostly short stories. This book is a compilation of his work.

The notion to write novels and pen his experiences took hold in a bar, in Bay City, Texas. He was having a few beers with Dorothy Housdorfer, his mentor and writing coach, and Carlos Ledson Miller, a successful writer from the Pacific side of the Canal Zone. After a round of storytelling, Carlos told him he needed to write down his experiences before old age robbed him of the memories.

Two years later, Arcia, frustrated with his inability to get published managed a lunch with Ray Fitzgerald, a friend and fellow member of The Woodlands Writers Guild, and Joe Lansdale, an accomplished writer from Nacogdoches, Texas. During the course of the meal, Arcia broke protocol and asked Joe for guidance. The advice given was, "If you want to get published, you must create a character, and find your own voice."

This direction proved fruitful. Arcia created Alex Perez, a lovable Panamanian scoundrel whose penchant for the female form lands him into all sorts of trouble. By writing in first person, and adding a bawdy style, he not only found his voice, but he developed a unique comedic flair that has served him well. His first novel, Cut and Run was picked-up by Arte Publico Press from Houston, Texas. It hit the market in November of 2009 - Buoyed by the success of the first one, two other Alex novels followed suit.

Arcia developed his particular knack for comedy from an enthusiastic admiration of Mae West, W.C. Fields, Benny Hill, John Cleese, and Peter Sellers. If you are familiar with these actors, you will clearly see their influence in his dialog, and in his comedy bravura.

Other Books by Alberto

Cut and Run – The Misadventures of Alex Perez is a picaresque novel in the style of Bob Hope & Bing Crosby's 'road' movies. The story follows Alex, a reluctant groom, as he travels from Mexico to Panama, with his future bride and odious mother-in-law. The story deals with the clash of cultures between north and south of the U.S. border, and exploits its idiosyncrasies. Rated M

In Search of High Ground – The Amorous Antics of Alex Perez is the story of an immoral man who tries to walk God's road. Alex, through a series of dreams is warned by the Almighty to behave or else. To encourage him, God shows Alex what heaven and hell will be for him. Wanting to save himself, he decides to head for high ground. However, salvation can only be his, if he's able to avoid the company of wanton women. Does he succeed? Rated R

**An Ill Wind That Blows No Good – Alex Perez'
Mexican Adventures** is a curious mix of facts and
fiction. The result is a hilarious, bawdy, story of a
Panamanian immigrant who decides to make
money by taking American tourists into Mexico on
Mayan Archeological Adventure tours. What
happens to him, his crew, and his customers makes
Murphy's Law look tame. In this one, Arcia brings
back most of the characters from the first two Alex
novels. Rated R

Alberto's works are available at Amazon and at
Createspace

83733775R00120

Made in the USA
Columbia, SC
26 December 2017